WHAT REVIEWERS ARE SAYING

"An emotionally smart gem of a book. *The Danish Way of Parenting* offers a shining alternative to high-stress modern parenting, and families from New Delhi to New York will shout with joy. Forget the pursuit of happiness, this book gets to the authentic roots of family happiness. I guess I'm Danish."

—Heather Shumaker, author of
It's OK Not to Share and *It's OK to Go Up the Slide*

"Everyone around the globe can gain something from the valuable wisdom found in this book. Concepts such as reframing and *hygge* prove useful to families from all cultures. It's wonderful to see that Danish parenting has so much in common with *Positive Parenting*! I highly recommend this book!"

—Rebecca Eanes, author of
Positive Parenting: An Essential Guide

"With a profound understanding of the positive impact that empathy and connectedness bring to parenting, *The Danish Way of Parenting* empowers parents across the globe to check their own default settings and consider the whole child. Their take on the importance of free play is a breath of fresh air in a time when young children are over-scheduled and under stress. Highly recommended for parents everywhere."

—Katie Hurley, LCSW, author of
The Happy Kid Handbook

"A powerful new method of raising children . . . who are 'resilient and emotionally secure'—in other words, exactly what we're all aiming for."

—*Mother* magazine

"Having studied the reasons behind the Danish happiness model for years, I found this book to be a clear-sighted, very useful, and smart guide on how to improve your own happiness level as a parent and how to foster happier children the Danish way. I would recommend this book to anyone who wants to give themselves and/or their children the best chances of a happy life."

—Malene Rydahl, keynote speaker and
Goodwill Ambassador of Copenhagen

"If the 'grown-ups' of every nation put the principles outlined in *The Danish Way* into practice even 50 percent of their waking lives, oh, the potential change to humanity. . . . Sometimes a book has the power to literally re-sculpt the world as we know it, bringing about changes to the next generation which could even make the word *war* a concept of the dim and distant past. *The Danish Way of Parenting* really is every adult's Bible."
—The Glass House Girls

"Nordic cuisine, Nordic design, Nordic Noir—the list of successful cultural exports has been a never-ending one over the last decade, and now you can add Nordic Nurture to the list. . . . It would appear that Danish mothers really do know best."
—*The Post* (Copenhagen)

"Alexander's research and honest reflection on how her own parenting has been influenced and enhanced by her husband's Danish culture is a valuable resource for any parent struggling to hold up a mirror to the vulnerabilities in his or her own parenting style. Sandahl's research and personal and professional experience as a Danish parent and psychotherapist reinforce the idea that Danes really do have some brilliant natural insight into raising resilient and balanced children. Together, the authors create a thoughtfully written parenting guide that encourages self-reflection and provides useful advice on how to best address common parenting challenges. *The Danish Way of Parenting* is a must-read for parents coming from any culture." —Carolyn Rathjen, MSW, LICSW

WHAT PARENTS ARE SAYING

"A book that makes the reader reflect. It isn't just about becoming a better parent but how you stand in the world, how you relate to others, and what kind of a person you want to be. I loved that angle to it!" —Karin W.

"This book stays with you, empowers you to find joy in the way we see ourselves and our children, with the hope our children will pass that lesson on when they become parents. Finally a deeply optimistic yet practical point of view." —Jason G.

"The idea that 'hygge' doesn't happen on its own but that you have to want it really stood out for me. I loved it!" —Kate H.

"The tips were great! I liked reading about the Danish kids' books. Kids should hear more about these not-so-easy topics through books because it gives parents a more comfortable space for teaching important life lessons. We often avoid hard or unpleasant topics with our kids (or partners) simply because we don't know what to say. It would make it much easier if the book was doing most of the talking!" —Jessica S.

THE DANISH WAY OF PARENTING

THE DANISH WAY
OF PARENTING

What the Happiest People in the World

Know About Raising Confident,

Capable Kids

JESSICA JOELLE ALEXANDER
and IBEN DISSING SANDAHL

A TarcherPerigee Book

An imprint of Penguin Random House LLC
375 Hudson Street
New York, New York 10014

Originally published by Jessica Joelle Alexander and Iben Dissing Sandahl 2014
This edition in slightly different form published by TarcherPerigee 2016

Most TarcherPerigee books are available at special quantity discounts for bulk
purchase for sales promotions, premiums, fund-raising, and educational needs.
Special books or book excerpts also can be created to fit specific needs. For
details, write: SpecialMarkets@penguinrandomhouse.com.

LIBRARY OF CONGRESS CATALOGING-IN-PUBLICATION DATA
Names: Alexander, Jessica Joelle, author. | Sandahl, Iben, author.
Title: The Danish way of parenting : what the happiest people in the world
know about raising confident, capable kids / Jessica Joelle Alexander and
Iben Sandahl.
Description: New York : TarcherPerigee, [2016] | Includes bibliographical
references and index.
Identifiers: LCCN 2016006963 (print) | LCCN 2016024358 (ebook) |
ISBN 9780143111719 | ISBN 9781101992975
Subjects: LCSH: Parenting—Denmark. | Parenting—Cross-cultural studies.
Classification: LCC HQ755.8 .A4395 2016 (print) | LCC HQ755.8 (ebook) |
DDC
306.874—dc23
LC record available at https://lccn.loc.gov/2016006963

Printed in the United States of America
15   17   19   20   18   16   14

Book design by Patrice Sheridan

Contents

Parent

———————— • ————————

Play Why free play creates happier, better adjusted, more resilient adults.

Authenticity Why honesty creates a stronger sense of self. How praise can be used to form a growth mind-set rather than a fixed mind-set, making your children more resilient.

Reframing Why reframing can change you and your children's lives for the better.

Empathy Why understanding, incorporating, and teaching empathy are fundamental in creating happier children and adults.

No Ultimatums Why avoiding power struggles and using a more democratic parenting approach fosters trust, resilience, and happier kids.

Togetherness and Hygge (Coziness) Why a strong social network is one of the most important factors in our overall happiness. How creating hygge (coziness) can help us give this powerful gift to our children.

———

Foreword to the Updated Edition

The process of researching and writing this book has truly been a labor of love. It all started with a question: *What makes Danish kids—and Danish parents—the happiest people on earth?*

As an American mom married to a Dane, and a Danish psychotherapist, both raising families of our own, the question was both deeply personal and intellectually fascinating. Uncovering the answers led us on a journey into research findings, facts about Denmark and interviews with professionals in a wide range of fields. When the first draft was completed, we sent it out to an informal focus group of moms, dads, and experts across the United States and Europe. This focus group encompassed Democrats and Republicans, granola moms and military dads, breast-feeders and spankers, attachment parents and tiger moms, from California to D.C. and beyond; we tried to reach every kind of parent from every walk of life possible.

Informed by their valuable feedback, we self-published the first edition of the book. We felt confident that we had created something special. However, we were still unprepared for the extraordinary journey it would take. From a grassroots movement to a growing global garden, it continues to humble us every day with each new reader.

When we initially put the book on the market and orders very languidly trickled in, we were bewildered by the locations of the sales: New Zealand, South Africa, various countries in Europe, Vietnam, Indonesia, Australia, and the United States, to name a few. Hollywood directors, Danish ambassadors, and college professors were buying the book. We knew this because we were physically packing, addressing, and mailing the books ourselves! This was promising, but it was also slow and tedious work, and the unlikelihood of success weighed upon us.

Slowly, however, we started hearing from readers—parents who were digesting our ideas and trying them out with their own families. This feedback from parents was more than just positive: It was full of gratitude and even relief that a parenting practice existed and furthermore supported a suspicion they had felt in their gut all along. A feeling that there must be another way to raise children, but one they had quashed due to societal expectations and pressure to do things "the right way."

Parents wrote us saying they loved the idea of focusing on play, empathy, and social skills—not just academics—as crucial elements to educating a child. And the fact that these practices were already in place in a thriving, happy society was eye-opening for many readers who hadn't heard much about Denmark before.

We discovered that the book was being used in colleges. One professor contacted us to tell us about a course she had created based on *The Danish Way of Parenting*—to rave reviews from her students, whose minds were opened to a different way of raising kids.

We continued to spread the word as much as possible about the value of the Danish Way, writing articles and doing interviews, and this began to have a domino effect.

A visiting Indian businessman bought the book on his way home from Denmark. He wrote to us that he wants to introduce *The Danish Way of Parenting* across India: into classes, pediatricians' offices, and teacher training programs as well as to the public at-large. "This is not a book," he wrote us, "it's a movement. And I see it as a movement to change a country." We were gratified beyond belief.

Now the book has landed in the hands of a major publisher in this updated edition. The rest of the story is history in the making.

Much like parenting, this book has been a difficult, arduous, joyful, and gratifying experience. The most rewarding and fulfilling aspect of it all, however, has been the incredible response from readers: the parents, grandparents, teachers and educators, the nonparents and psychologists, the book clubs, and general word of mouth. Whether people have agreed with every aspect of the Danish Way or not, it has certainly been a conversation starter. These ideas have been the seeds of a grassroots movement and helped it grow into what it is today. We hope these ideas, like seeds, will continue to spread on the wind so that more kindness, empathy, and happiness will flourish across the world. And we hope they'll bring greater happiness to you and your family too.

Jessica Joelle Alexander
Iben Dissing Sandahl
Copenhagen
February 2016

Introduction

•

What's the Secret to Danish Happiness?

Denmark, a small country in the north of Europe famous for Hans Christian Andersen's fairy tale "The Little Mermaid," has been voted as having the happiest people in the world by the OECD (Organisation for Economic Co-operation and Development) almost every year since 1973. 1973! That's more than forty years of consistently being voted the happiest people in the world! If you stop to think about that for a second, it's a staggering accomplishment. Even the new *World Happiness Report* that was recently launched by the United Nations has seen Denmark top the list every year since its inception. What is the secret to their consistent success?

Countless articles and studies have been devoted to solving this mystery. Denmark? Why Denmark? *60 Minutes* did a report on it called "The Pursuit of Happiness"; Oprah did a show on it, "Why Are the Danes So Happy?" and the conclusions are always conveniently inconclusive. Is it the size of their social system, their houses, or their government? It can't be the high taxes or the cold, dark winters, so what gives?

The United States, on the other hand, the country with "the pursuit of happiness" built into its Declaration of Independence, isn't even in the top ten. It's barely in the top twenty, closer to number seventeen after Mexico. Despite having an entire field of psychology devoted to happiness and an endless sea of self-help books instructing us on how to attain this elusive state, we aren't really that happy. Why is that? And moreover, why are the Danes so content?

After many years of research, we think we have finally uncovered the secret of why the Danes are so happy. And the answer, quite simply, is in their upbringing.

The Danish philosophy behind parenting and their way of raising children yields some pretty powerful results: resilient, emotionally secure, happy kids who turn into resilient, emotionally secure, happy adults who then repeat this powerful parenting style with their own kids. The legacy repeats itself, and we get a society that tops the happiness charts for more than forty years in a row.

Through this amazing journey of discovery, we have decided to share this knowledge about "the Danish Way" of parenting with you. In this step-by-step guide, our goal is to help mothers and fathers who are about to embark on or have already begun one of the most challenging and extraordinary jobs in the world. Incorporating this method takes practice, patience, resolve, and awareness, but the outcome is well worth the work. Remember that this is your legacy. If your goal is to raise the happiest people in the world, then please read on. The real secret of the Danes' success is inside.

Jessica's Story

When my friends heard that I had cowritten a parenting book, they all laughed. "You, the most nonmaternal woman we know, cowrote a parenting book?" The irony is, it was precisely my lack of natural mothering skills that made me so interested in the Danish Way in the first place. It had changed my life so profoundly that I knew if it could help me, it could definitely help others.

You see, I wasn't born with all those innate nurturing mother skills supposedly all women are born with. I don't have a problem admitting it. I wasn't a kid person. I didn't even like kids that much, if I am to be completely honest. I became a mom because that's what people do. So you can imagine my deep-seated fear when I got pregnant and thought, "How in the world am I going to do this? Surely I am going to be a terrible mom!" And so I got busy reading every parenting book I could get my hands on. I read a lot. I learned a lot. But still, the fear remained.

To my good fortune, I was married to a Dane. For more than eight years I had been exposed to the Danish culture, and one thing I noticed was that they were clearly doing something right with their children. Overall, I consistently observed happy, calm, well-behaved kids, and I wondered what their secret was. But there was no parenting book I could find on the subject.

When I finally became a mother, I found myself doing the only natural thing for me, which was to ask my Danish friends and family for every single answer to every single question I had. From breast-feeding to discipline to education, I preferred their off-the-cuff answers to all the books I had on my shelf. Through this journey, I discovered a philosophy of raising children that opened my eyes and changed my life completely.

My good friend Iben and I discussed the idea. Iben is a Danish psychotherapist with many years of experience working with families and children, and together we asked the question, "Does a Danish way of parenting exist?" To her knowledge, it didn't. We looked high and low for some literature on the subject, but there was nothing. In all her years working in the Danish school system and being a family psychotherapist, she had never heard of a "Danish Way." She knew all the academic theories and the research on parenting practices, many of which she used in her family life on a daily basis, but could there be a distinctive parenting style embedded in her very own culture that she hadn't seen?

A Pattern Emerges

The more we talked about it, the more it became clear that there was indeed a Danish parenting philosophy, but it was woven so tightly into the fabric of daily life and Danish culture that it wasn't immediately visible to those of us in the midst of it. The more we looked at it, the more the pattern emerged from the fabric. And there it was, laid out before us: *The Danish Way of Parenting.*

The Danish Way is our theory based on our more than thirteen years of experience, research, supporting studies, and facts about Danish culture and daily life. Iben is an expert in her field, bringing professional insight as well as many supporting studies and cultural examples, along with her personal experience. We have both learned so much along this journey, having researched and conducted extensive interviews with parents, psychologists, and teachers regarding the Danish school system. The collaboration was wholly equal, and all the supporting studies can be found in the back of the book.

> Happy kids grow up to be happy adults who raise happy kids, and so on.

We would like to clarify that this is not a political statement, nor is it a book about living in Denmark. It is a parenting theory, which we believe is one of the leading factors as to why the Danes are voted so consistently happy. Happy kids grow up to be happy adults who raise happy kids, and so on.

We also know that parenting style is not the only reason the Danes are happy. We know there are many factors contributing to their happiness and that there are certainly unhappy people living there as well. Denmark is not utopia, and surely it has its own internal matters to deal with, as does every country. Nor is this book in any way meant to be disparaging to the U.S. This is an enormous country, and the facts and observations we state in the book are generalizations. Jessica, personally, is very proud to be American and loves her country dearly. She has simply had the opportunity to see the world with a very different pair of glasses on—through "Danish lenses," if you will—and it has changed her whole perspective on life.

We would like to offer you these glasses to put on for yourself and see what you think when you look through them. If this book helps you see things differently, then, for us, it has been a success. You might not go from "the most nonmaternal person" to a happier parent and better human being, as Jessica has, but we hope the changes will be positive ones. And we hope you will enjoy the journey.

CHAPTER 1

Recognizing Our
Default Settings

We have all thought from time to time about what it means to be a parent. Whether it's before the birth of your first child, during a toddler meltdown, or during a fight at the dinner table over your child not eating his or her peas, we have all once thought, "Am I doing this right?" Many of us refer to books and the Internet, or we talk to friends and family for advice and support. Most of us just want to be reassured that we are, in fact, doing things the right way.

But have you ever considered what the right way is? Where do we get our ideas about the right way of parenting? If you go to Italy, you will see children eating dinner at nine p.m. and running around in restaurants until almost midnight; in Norway babies are regularly left outside in minus-twenty-degree weather to sleep; and in Belgium kids are allowed to drink beer. To us, some of these behaviors seem bizarre, but to these parents it is the "right" way.

These implicit, taken-for-granted ideas we have about how to raise our children are what Sara Harkness, a professor of human development at the University of Connecticut, calls "parental ethnotheories." She has studied this phenomenon for decades across cultures, and what she has found is that these intrinsic beliefs about the right way to parent are so ingrained in our society that it's almost impossible to see them objectively. For us, it just seems to be the way things are.

And so, most of us have thought about what it means to be a parent, but have you ever thought about what it means to be an American parent? About how the American glasses we wear color our ability to see what "the right way" is?

What if we were to take those glasses off for a moment—what would we see? If we stood back and looked at the U.S. from a distance, what would our impression be?

An Epidemic of Stress

For years we have seen a growing problem with people's happiness level across the board in the United States. Antidepressant use went up 400 percent between 2005 and 2008, according to the National Center for Health Statistics. Children are being diagnosed with and prescribed medication for a growing number of psychological disorders, some with no clear-cut method of diagnosis. In 2010 alone, there were at least 5.2 million children between the ages of three and seventeen taking Ritalin for attention deficit disorder.

We are fighting obesity and early onset of puberty, or "precocious puberty," as it is now called. Girls and boys as young as seven and eight are getting injected with hormone shots to stop puberty. Most of us don't even question this as strange; rather, it's just the way things are. "My daughter is getting the shot," one mother recently rattled off nonchalantly about her eight-year-old, who she thought was hitting puberty too soon.

Many parents are excessively competitive with themselves, with their children, and with other parents without even realizing it. Of course, not all people are like this, nor do they want to be, but they can also feel pressured living in this competitive culture. The language surrounding them can be intense and challenging, putting people on the defensive: "Kim is just amazing at soccer. The coach says she is one of the best on the team. But she is still managing straight A's despite soccer, karate, and swimming. I don't know how she does it! What about Olivia? How is she doing?" We feel pressure to perform—for our kids to perform, to do well in school and fulfill our idea of what a successful kid should be, what a successful parent should be. Stress levels are often high, and we feel judged—by others and by ourselves. Part of this is human nature, and part of it is what it is to be American. What is pushing us as a society to perform and compete and be successful to a standard that ultimately doesn't seem to be making us very happy as adults? What if some of the "answers" we have for raising our kids—our parental norms—are flawed?

What if we discovered that the glasses we were wearing had the wrong prescription and we weren't able to see things as clearly as we thought? We would change the lenses, correcting our vision, and look again at our world. Lo and behold, we'd find that things do look different! By trying to see things from a new perspective, with new lenses, the question arises naturally: *Is there a better way?*

Examining Our "Default Settings"

The other day, Jessica was in the city with her almost-three-year-old son. He was on a push-bike with no pedals, and he started to push himself out toward the street despite her yelling at him numerous times to stop. She ran after him frantically, grabbing him hard by the arm and giving him a shake. She was furious and scared, and was about to yell, "You'd better stop when I tell you to stop!" Jessica could see he was going to cry out of fear, and in that moment, it took all of her might to muster up the strength to go outside herself and observe what she was doing. That wasn't how she wanted to react. She scanned her mind for another way and, miraculously, an answer was there. She stopped, took a breath, and got down on his level. She held his arms and looked into his eyes imploringly. In a calm but concerned voice, she said, "Do you want to go ow-ow? Mommy doesn't want you to go ow-ow! Do you see those cars?" She pointed to the cars and he nodded. "Cars go ow-ow to Sebastian!"

He nodded, listening to her. "Cars. Ow-ow," he repeated.

"So when Mommy says to stop, you stop, OK? So that you don't go ow-ow from the cars."

He nodded. He didn't cry in the end. They hugged, and Jessica could feel him nodding on her shoulder. "Cars. Ow-ow."

Five minutes later they were at another crosswalk. Jessica told him to stop, and he did. He pointed to the road and shook his head. "Cars ow-ow." She showed him how happy she was by jumping up and down and clapping. She wasn't just happy with him for stopping, you see. She was also happy with *herself* for stopping—for stopping herself and changing her natural behavior, her default settings, in a difficult moment. It wasn't easy, but doing this turned a stressful and potentially explosive situation into a joyful and safe one, and the results made them both happier for it.

Sometimes we forget that parenting, like love, is a verb. It takes effort and work to yield positive returns. There is an incredible amount of self-awareness involved in being a good parent. It requires us to look at what we do when we are tired and stressed and stretched to our limits. These actions are called our "default settings." Our default settings are the actions and reactions we have when we are too tired to choose a better way.

> Sometimes we forget that parenting, like love, is a verb.

Most of our default settings are inherited from our own parents. They are ingrained and programmed into us like a motherboard on a computer. They are the factory settings we return to when we are at our wit's end and not thinking; they have been installed in us by our upbringing. It's when we hear ourselves saying things we don't really want to be saying. It's when we act and react in ways we aren't sure we want to be acting and reacting. It's when we feel bad because deep down we know there is a better way to get results from our kids, but we aren't sure what it is. Anyone who has kids is familiar with this feeling.

That's why it is so important to look at your default settings, study them, and understand them. What do you like about how you act and react with your children? What don't you like? What are you doing that is just a repeat from your own upbringing? What would you like to change? Only when you see what your natural inclinations as a parent—your default settings—are can you decide how you want to change them for the better.

In the chapters that follow, we'll help you see what some of those positive changes can be. Using the easy-to-remember acronym PARENT—play, authenticity, reframing, empathy, no ultimatums, and togetherness—we'll examine some of the tried-and-true methods that have been working for parents in Denmark for more than forty years.

Increasing our self-awareness and making conscious decisions about our actions and reactions are the first steps toward powerful life change. This is how we become better parents—and better people. And this is how we create a legacy of well-being to pass on to the next generations. Is there a greater gift you can give to your children and your children's children than helping them grow up to be happier, more secure and resilient adults? We don't think so. And we hope you'll agree.

CHAPTER 2

P Is for Play

Play is often talked about as if it were a relief from serious learning, but for children play is serious learning.

MR. ROGERS

Have you noticed that there is an unspoken or even spoken pressure to organize activities for your kids? Whether it's swimming, ballet, T-ball, or soccer, somehow you just don't feel like you are doing your job if you don't have your kids signed up for at least three or four things a week. How many times do you hear parents saying that their Saturday is taken up with driving their children to various sports, lessons, or activities?

In contrast, when was the last time you heard someone say, "On Saturday, my daughter is going to play"?

And by "play," we don't mean play the violin or play a sport or even go on a playdate in which adults have organized activities. We mean "play" in which they are left to their own devices, with a friend or alone, to play exactly as they see fit, for as long as they want. And even if parents do allow this free play to take place, there is often a nagging feeling of guilt about admitting it. Because, ultimately, we feel we are being better parents by teaching them something, having them involved in a sport, or giving their little brains some input. Play often seems like a waste of valuable learning time. But is it?

In the United States in the past fifty years, the number of hours that children are allowed to play has decreased dramatically. Aside from television and technology, there is also parents' fear of kids getting hurt coupled with a desire to "develop" them—all these factors have taken over much of the time they once had to play.

As parents, we feel comforted when our children are making visible signs of progress. We like watching them play soccer while others cheer them on, or going to their ballet or piano recitals. We feel proud to say that Billy won a medal or a trophy or learned a new song or can recite the alphabet in Spanish. It makes us feel like we are good parents. We do it with the best intentions because by giving them more instruction and structured activities, we are giving them training to become more successful, thriving adults. Or are we?

It's no secret that the diagnosis of anxiety disorders, depression, and attention disorders has skyrocketed in the U.S. Is it possible that we are making our kids anxious without realizing it by not allowing them to play more?

Are We Overprogramming Our Kids' Lives?

Many parents strive to start their children at school early or jump a grade. Kids learn to read and do math earlier and earlier and we are proud because they are "smart," and being smart or athletic are highly valued characteristics in American culture. We may go to great lengths with tutors and educational toys and programs to try to get them there. Success is success and these are tangible, visible, measurable signs. Free play, for all intents and purposes, seems fun—but what is it really teaching them?

What if we told you that free play teaches children to be less anxious? It teaches them resilience. And resilience has been proven to be one of the most important factors in predicting success as an adult. The ability to "bounce back," regulate emotions, and cope with stress is a key trait in a healthy, functioning adult. We now know that resilience is great for preventing anxiety and depression, and it's something the Danes have been instilling in their children for years. And one of the ways they have done it is by placing a lot of importance on play.

> Free play teaches children to be less anxious.

In Denmark, dating back to 1871, husband and wife Niels and Erna Juel-Hansen came up with the first pedagogy based on educational theory, which incorporated play. They discovered that free play is crucial for a child's development. In fact, for many years, Danish children weren't even allowed to start school before they were seven. Educators and people who set the agenda for children's schooling didn't want them to engage in education because they felt that children should first and foremost be children and play. Even now, children age ten and under finish regular school at two p.m. and then have the option to go to what is called "free-time school" (*skolefritidsordning*) for the rest of the day, where they are mainly encouraged to play. Amazing but true!

In Denmark, there isn't a sole emphasis on education or sports, but rather on the whole child. Parents and teachers focus on things like socialization, autonomy, cohesion, democracy, and self-esteem. They want their children to learn resilience and develop a strong internal compass to guide them through life. They know their kids will be well educated and learn many skills. But true happiness isn't coming only from a good education. A child who learns to cope with stress, makes friends, and yet is realistic about the world has a set of life skills that are very different from being a math genius, for example. And by life skills, the Danes are talking about all aspects of life, not only career life. For what is a math genius without the ability to cope with life's ups and downs? All the Danish parents we spoke to said that excessive focus on pressuring young children seemed very strange to them.

As they see it, if children are always performing in order to obtain something—good grades, awards, or praise from teachers or parents—then they don't get to develop their inner drive. They believe that children fundamentally need space and trust to allow them to master things by themselves, to make and solve their own problems. This creates genuine self-esteem and self-reliance because it comes from the child's own internal cheerleader, not from someone else.

Internal vs. External Locus of Control

In psychology, this internal cheerleader or drive is known as the locus of control. The word *locus* in Latin means "place" or "location," and so the locus of control simply refers to the degree to which a person feels he has a sense of control over his own life and the events that affect him. Thus, people with an internal locus of control believe that they have the power to control their lives and the things that happen to them. Their drive is internal, or personal; their place of control comes from the inside. People with an external locus of control believe that their lives are controlled by external factors such as the environment or fate, which they have little influence over. What drives them is coming from the outside, and they can't change it. We are all affected by our surroundings, culture, and social status, but how much we feel we can control our lives despite those factors is the difference between internal and external locus of control.

Studies have repeatedly shown that children, adolescents, and adults who have a strong external locus of control are predisposed to anxiety and depression—they become anxious because they believe they have little or no control over their fate, and they become depressed when this sense of helplessness gets to be too great.

Research also shows that there has been a dramatic shift toward a more external locus of control among young people in the past fifty years. Psychologist Jean M. Twenge and colleagues examined results from a test called the Children's Nowicki-Strickland Internal-External Control Scale over a fifty-year period. This test measures whether a person has an internal or an external locus of control. The researchers discovered that there was a dramatic shift from an internal to an external locus of control in children of all ages, from elementary school to college. To give you an idea of how great a shift it was, young people in 1960 were 80 percent more likely to claim that they had control over their lives than children in 2002, who were more prone to say they lacked such personal control.

And what was even more striking was that the trend was more pronounced for elementary school children than for middle school and college kids. So younger and younger children are feeling a lack of control over their lives. They are feeling this sense of helplessness earlier and earlier. This rise in external locus of control over the years has a linear correlation with the rise in depression and anxiety in our society. What could be causing this shift?

Giving Kids the Space to Learn and Grow

Central to the Danish parenting philosophy is a concept called "proximal development," first introduced by Lev Vygotsky, a Russian developmental psychologist. This basically states that a child needs the right amount of space to learn and grow in the zones that are right for him or her, with the right amount of help. Imagine helping a child climb over a fallen log in the forest. If at first he needs a hand, you give the hand, but then perpaps only a finger to help him over, and when it is time, you let him go. You don't carry or push him over. In Denmark, parents try not to intervene unless it's absolutely necessary. They trust their children to be able to do and try new things and give them space to build their own trust in themselves. They provide them with scaffolding for their development and help them build their self-esteem, which is very important for the "whole child." If children feel too pressured, they can lose the joy in what they are doing, and this can lead to fear and anxiety. Instead, Danish parents try to meet children where they feel secure trying a new skill, and then challenge and invite them to go further or try something new, while it still feels exciting and strange.

> In Denmark, parents try not to intervene unless it's absolutely necessary.

Giving this space and respecting the zone of proximal development allows children to develop both competence and confidence in their internal locus of control because they feel they are in charge of their own challenges and development. Children who are pushed or pulled too much risk developing an external locus of control because they aren't controlling their development; instead, external factors are, and the foundation for their self-esteem becomes shaky.

We sometimes think we are helping kids by pushing them

to perform or learn faster, but leading them in the right moment of their development will yield much better results—not only because of the learning itself, which will surely be more pleasurable, but because the children will be more assured of the mastery of their skills, since they feel more in charge of acquiring them.

David Elkind, an American psychologist, agrees. Children who are pushed to read earlier, for example, may read better than their peers initially, but those levels even out in a few years' time—and at what cost? The pushed children exhibit higher levels of anxiety and lower self-esteem in the long run.

In the U.S., we find an endless number of books on how to lower or reduce anxiety and stress. We want to eliminate stress at all costs, particularly for our children. Many parents helicopter over their children and intervene to protect them at a moment's notice. Most of us barricade staircases and protect and lock up anything we can find that might be remotely dangerous. If we don't, we feel we are being bad parents and, in fact, we judge and are judged by others for not doing enough to protect them. These days require so many safeguarding gizmos and gadgets that one wonders how children survived twenty years ago.

Not only do we want to protect our children from stress, but we also want to build their self-confidence and make them feel special. The standard method of doing this is to praise them, sometimes excessively, for insignificant accomplishments. But in our quest to increase confidence and reduce stress, we may actually be setting them up for more stress in the long run. Building confidence rather than self-esteem is like making a nice house with little foundation. We all know what happens when the big bad wolf comes.

But How Can Play Help?

Scientists have been studying play in animals for years, trying to understand its evolutionary purpose. And one thing they are finding is that play is crucial for learning how to cope with stress. In studies done on domestic rats and rhesus monkeys, scientists found that when they were deprived of playmates during a critical stage of their development, these animals became stressed out as adults. They would overreact to challenging situations and were unable to cope well in social settings. They would react either with excessive fear, sometimes running shaking into a corner, or with exaggerated aggression, lashing out in rage. The lack of play was definitely the culprit, because when the animals were allowed a playmate for even an hour a day, they developed more normally and coped better as adults.

Fight-or-flight behaviors, normally experienced in play, activate the same neurochemical pathways in the brain as stress does. Think about when you see dogs running around chasing each other for fun. Many animals engage in this kind of play, taking the subordinate or attacker position in a play fight, creating a kind of stress. We know that exposing the brains of baby animals to stress changes them in a way that makes them less responsive to stress over time, meaning that the more they play, the better their brains become at regulating stress as they grow. Their ability to cope improves constantly through playing, and they are able to deal with more and more difficult situations. Resilience isn't cultivated by avoiding stress, you see, but by learning how to tame and master it.

Are we taking away our kids' ability to regulate stress by not allowing them to play enough? Looking at the number of anxiety disorders and diagnoses of depression in our society, one wonders if something is amiss. Since one of the biggest reported fears of someone with an anxiety disorder is losing control of one's emotions, we can't help but ask: If we stand back and let our children play more, will they be more resilient and happier adults? We think the answer is yes.

Play and Coping Skills

In a pilot study conducted on preschool children in a child development center in Massachusetts, researchers wanted to measure whether there was a positive correlation between the level of playfulness in preschoolers and their coping skills. Using a test of playfulness and a coping inventory, the researchers cross-checked the children's playfulness and the quality of their coping skills. What they found was that there was a direct positive correlation between children's playfulness level and their ability to cope. The more they played—that is, the better they became at learning social skills and engaging in social/play contexts—the better they were at coping. This led the researchers to believe that play had a direct effect on all of their life adaptability skills.

Another study, conducted by occupational therapy professor Louise Hess and colleagues at a health institute in Palo Alto, California, sought to investigate the relationship between playfulness and coping skills in adolescent boys. They studied both normally developing boys and those with emotional problems. As in the preschool study, for both groups of boys there was a direct and significant correlation between the level of playfulness and their ability to cope. The researchers concluded that play could be employed to improve coping skills, particularly the abilities to adapt and to approach problems and goals in a more flexible way.

This makes sense. Just look outside to see children swinging from bars or climbing trees or jumping from high places. They are testing dangerous situations, and no one but the child himself knows the right dose or how to manage it. But it's important that they feel in control of the dose of stress they can handle. This in itself makes them feel more in control of their lives. Juvenile animals and primates do the same thing. They deliberately put themselves into dangerous situations, leaping and swinging from trees while twisting and turning and making it difficult to land. They are learning about fear and how to cope with it. It's the same with play fighting, as mentioned earlier. The animals are putting themselves into both the subordinate and the attacker positions to understand the emotional challenges of both.

For children, social situations are also stressful. Social play can bring on both conflict and cooperation. Fear and anger are just some of the emotions that a child must learn to cope with in order to keep playing. In play there is no such thing as getting excessive praise. Rules have to be negotiated and renegotiated, and players have to be aware of the emotional state of the other players in order to avoid someone getting upset and quitting, because if too many players quit, the game is over. Since children fundamentally want to play with each other, these situations require them to practice getting along with others as equals—a vital skill for happiness in later life.

Play is so central to the Danish view of childhood that many Danish schools have programs in place to promote learning through sports, play, and exercise for all students. Play Patrol, for example, is focused on the youngest elementary school students, and is facilitated by the older ones. These student-led programs encourage both young and older students to play various activities such as hide-and-seek, firefighter, or family pet—and to encourage shy, lonely kids to join in the game too. This type of fun and imaginative play, with mixed age groups, encourages kids to test themselves in a way they wouldn't with their parents or teachers. It greatly reduces bullying and further fosters social skills and self-control.

The Truth Behind Lego and Playgrounds

Almost everyone has heard of Lego and played with the famous colorful building blocks at least once in their lives. Ostensibly one of the most popular toys in history, Lego was dubbed "the toy of the century" by *Fortune* magazine at the start of the millennium. Originally made from wood, Lego has never lost its fundamental building-block concept. Like the zone of proximal development, Lego can work for all ages. When the child is ready to take the next step toward a more challenging construction, there are Legos made for doing so. It's a wonderful way to play with your child to gently help her master a new level. She can play on her own or with friends; countless hours have been spent playing with Lego all over the world.

The interesting fact most people don't know about Lego is that it comes from Denmark. Created by a Danish carpenter in his workshop in 1932, it was called Lego as a contraction of the words *leg godt*, which means "play well." Even then, the idea of using your imagination to play freely was in full bloom.

Another of the world's biggest suppliers of play facilitators is another Danish company called Kompan. It creates outdoor playgrounds that have won numerous design awards for their simplicity, quality, and functionality in supporting children's play. The company's mission has been to promote healthy play as important for children's learning. Its first playground was developed accidentally more than forty years ago when a young Danish artist noticed that his colorful art installation, created to brighten up a drab housing facility, was used more by children to play on than for the admiration of adults.

Kompan is now the number one playground supplier in the world. It's notable and quite telling that a country of only five million people is the world leader in both indoor and outdoor play supplies.

So the next time you see your children swinging from the branches, jumping off some rocks, or play fighting with their friends and you want to intervene to save them, remember that this is their way of learning how much stress they can endure. When they are playing in a group with some difficult children and you want to protect them, remember that they are learning self-control and negotiation skills with all kinds of different personalities to keep the game alive. This is their way of testing their own abilities and developing adaptability skills in the process. The more they play, the more resilient and socially adept they will become. It's a very natural process. Being able to *leg godt* or "play well" is the building block to creating an empire of future happiness.

> The more they play, the more resilient and socially adept they will become.

Tips for Play

1. Turn it off

Turn off the TV and the electronics! Imagination is an essential ingredient for play to have its positive effects.

2. Create an enriching environment

Studies show that a sensory-rich environment coupled with play facilitates cortical growth in the brain. Having a variety of materials around that can stimulate all of the senses—visual, auditory, tactile, and so on—enhances brain development during play.

3. Use art

Children's brains grow when they make art. Therefore, don't show them how to do it—just put out the art supplies and let them create spontaneously.

4. Let them explore outside

Get them outside as much as possible to play in nature—the woods, the park, the beach, wherever. Try to find safe areas where you aren't afraid to let them be free and explore the environment. These are places they can really use their imaginations and have fun.

5. Mix children of different ages

Try to mix your children with children of different ages. This enhances the zone of proximal development, allowing one to facilitate the other's learning, helping each get to a new level naturally. In this way, children learn to both star in the game as well as co-operate with the older ones. They learn to participate as well as challenge the game. This is teaching the self-control and negotiation skills so necessary in life.

6. Let them be free and forget the guilt

They don't need an adult-led activity or specific toys. The more you can let them be in control of their own play, using their imagination and doing it themselves, the better they will get at it. The skills they are learning are invaluable. We are so caught up in worrying about how many organized activities our children are involved in or what they are learning that we are forgetting the importance of letting them play freely. Stop feeling guilty that letting them play means you aren't parenting. Free play is what they are missing!

7. Be real

If you want to play with your kids, you must be 100 percent real in what you do. Don't be afraid to look silly. Let them guide. Stop worrying about what others think of you or what you think of yourself. Get down on their level and try to let go for even twenty minutes a day if this is difficult for you. Even a little playtime on their level is worth more than any toy you could buy.

8. Let them play alone too

Playing alone is extremely important for kids. When they play with their toys, it is often their way of processing new experiences, conflicts, and everyday events in their lives. By engaging in fantasy play and using different voices, they can reenact what is happening in their world, which is hugely therapeutic. It is also great for developing their fantasy and imagination.

9. **Create an obstacle course**

   Try building obstacle courses with small stools and mattresses, or by any other means create space in the home so that children can move about and use their imagination. Let them be free to play and climb and explore and create—and don't stress over it.

10. **Get other parents involved**

    Get other parents involved in the healthy play movement. The more parents who practice it, the more kids can be free to play together in non-adult-led activities. Pediatricians in the U.S. have developed guidelines to persuade parents that play is healthy. It is valuable for children and should be encouraged and discussed with others.

11. **Avoid intervening too quickly**

    Try not to judge the other kids too harshly and intervene too quickly because you want to protect your kids from others. Sometimes it is learning how to deal with the more difficult children that provides them the biggest lessons in self-control and resilience.

12. Let go

Let your kids do things by themselves. When you feel the need to "save" them, step back and take a breath. Remember that they are learning some of the most important skills to take them through life.

CHAPTER 3

---•---

A Is for Authenticity

No legacy is so rich as honesty.

WILLIAM SHAKESPEARE

Have you ever watched a feel-good movie with a happy ending that didn't actually leave you feeling good? One in which, despite the great ending, you noticed that somewhere deep inside yourself you had the inkling that your life wasn't that great? Your job wasn't that great? Your relationship, your house, your car, or your clothes just weren't as good as those in the film? The whole thing actually didn't feel that realistic? But you push it aside because, after all, it was a feel-good film, so no need to think too much about it. Most Hollywood films are intended to make you feel good. But if art imitates life, one wonders how realistic these syrupy-sweet endings actually are.

Danish films, on the other hand, very often have dreary, sad, or tragic endings. Much more rarely is one left with the happy endings we are accustomed to. Many times, Jessica has watched Danish films and waited to hear that soothing background music that would signal that her suffering was about to end and everything would turn out all right after all. The boy would get the girl, the hero would save the day, and all would be right with the world. As an American, she almost felt it was her right to have a happy ending. But time and time again, the Danish films would touch on sensitive, real, and painful issues that didn't wrap it up with a nice bow. On the contrary, they left Jessica and her fellow audience members alone with their raw emotions activated and unresolved. How could Danes be so happy watching films like this?

Communications professor Silvia Knobloch-Westerwick and colleagues at Ohio State University have done research that has demonstrated that, contrary to popular belief, watching tragic or sad movies actually makes people happier by bringing attention to some of the more positive aspects of their own lives. It tends to make people reflect on their own relationships with gratitude and perspective, leaving us feeling enriched and more in touch with our own humanity.

Fairy-tale Endings

Hans Christian Andersen is perhaps one of the most famous Danish writers in history. He is the author and forefather of numerous fairy tales such as "The Little Mermaid," "The Ugly Duckling," and "The Emperor's New Clothes," just to name a few. These are tales that have been told the world over. But what most people don't realize is that a lot of Andersen's original fairy tales don't have our idea of a fairy-tale ending at all. They are tragedies. The Little Mermaid, for example, doesn't get the prince but instead turns into sea foam because of sadness. Many of Andersen's fairy tales have merely been tailored to fit our cultural ideal of how things should be.

In the English translations of Andersen's fairy tales, adults have paid close attention to what they think children should be spared from hearing. In Denmark and in older versions, it is more up to the readers to come up with their own conclusions and judgments. Danes believe that tragedies and upsetting events are things we should talk about too. We learn more about character from our sufferings than from our successes; therefore, it's important to examine all parts of life. This is more authentic, and it creates empathy and a deeper respect for humanity. It also helps us feel gratitude for the simple things in our lives we sometimes take for granted by focusing too much on the fairy-tale life.

For Danes, authenticity begins with an understanding of our own emotions. If we teach our children to recognize and accept their authentic feelings, good or bad, and act in a way that's consistent with their values, the challenges and rough patches in life won't topple them. They will know that they have acted in accordance with what feels right. They will know how to recognize their own limits and respect them. This inner compass, an authentic self-esteem based on values, becomes the most powerful guiding force in one's life, largely resistant to external pressures.

Parenting with Authenticity

Parenting with authenticity is the first step to guiding children to be courageously true to themselves and others. Being a model of emotional health is powerful parenting. Emotional honesty, not perfection, is what children truly need from their parents. Children are always observing how you feel anger, joy, frustration, contentment, and success and how you express it in the world. We have to model honesty for our children and let them know that it is OK to feel all of their emotions. Many parents find it easier to manage their children's happy feelings, but when it comes to the more challenging ones, such as anger, aggression, and anxiety, it becomes more difficult. Therefore, children learn less about these emotions, which may affect their ability to regulate them in the future. Acknowledging and accepting all emotions, even the hard ones, early on makes it easier to maneuver in the world.

When going through a difficult time, for example, smiling and saying everything is OK is not always the best course of action. Self-deception is the worst kind of deception and is a dangerous message to send to our kids. They will learn to do the same. Self-deception is confusing because it makes us ignore our real feelings and can cause us to make choices based on external influences rather than on our own authentic desires. This leads us down paths to places we don't actually want to be in life. And that is how we end up unhappy. It's that moment when many people look at their lives and say, "Hold on, is this what I really wanted? Or is this what I thought I was supposed to want?"

In contrast, authenticity is searching your heart and gut for what is right for you and your family and not being afraid to follow through with it. It's allowing yourself to be in touch with your own emotions and act on them rather than burying or numbing them. These things take courage and strength, but the payoff is huge. Learning to act on intrinsic goals, such as improving relationships or engaging in hobbies you love, rather than on extrinsic goals, such as buying a new car, is what is proven to create true well-being.

Thus, having the bigger house or more stuff or enrolling your kids in all the right activities can be a self-deceptive pitfall. Pushing your own or others' dreams onto your kids, rather than listening carefully to their desires and respecting their unique pace of growth and development, is another pitfall. Being too pressured or praised, children may learn to do things for external recognition rather than for internal satisfaction, which becomes a default setting for life. It encourages extrinsic goals: needing something outside themselves to make them happy. This may bring success by some people's standards, but it won't necessarily bring them that deep sense of internal happiness and well-being we are all striving for. As we saw earlier, it can actually breed anxiety and depression.

The Danish Way of
Authentic Praise

Being humble is a very important value in Denmark. This dates far back in history and is a part of the Danes' cultural heritage. This value of humility is about knowing who you are so well that you don't need others to make you feel important. Therefore, they try not to overload their children with compliments.

Iben often tells her daughters they can do anything with hard work. They know they have to develop themselves and grow, and she encourages that. But she tries not to overpraise them, believing that kids can't make sense of too many compliments because they can sound empty and hollow.

For example, if a Danish child scribbles a drawing very quickly and gives it to her parent, the parent probably wouldn't say, "Wow! Great job! You are such a good artist!" She is more likely to ask about the drawing itself. "What is it?" "What were you thinking about when you drew this?" "Why did you use those colors?" Or perhaps she would just say thank you if it was a gift.

Focusing on the task, rather than overcomplimenting the child, is a much more Danish approach. This helps to focus on the work involved, but it also teaches humility. Helping children build on the feeling of being able to master a skill rather than already being a master provides a more solid foundation to stand on and grow from. This promotes inner strength and resilience.

And, in fact, new and very interesting research supports this idea. The way we praise our children does have a profound effect on resilience!

Fixed Mind-set vs. a Growth Mind-set

In the U.S., many parents believe that praising kids for how smart they are builds their confidence and motivation to learn. American parents tend to freely praise their children and others, believing it helps their confidence and development. But three decades of research done by Stanford psychologist Carol S. Dweck has proven otherwise.

Praise is closely connected to how kids view their intelligence. If they are constantly praised for being naturally smart, talented, or gifted (sound familiar?), they develop what is called a "fixed" mind-set (their intelligence is fixed and they have it).

In contrast, children who are told that their intelligence can be developed with work and education develop a growth mind-set (they can develop their skills because they are working very hard).

Dweck's findings show that kids who have a fixed mind-set, who have constantly been told they are smart, tend to care first and foremost about how they will be judged: smart or not smart. They become afraid to have to exert too much effort because effort makes them feel dumb. They believe that if you have the ability, you shouldn't need to put in the effort. And since they have always been told they have the ability, they are afraid that by needing to really try hard to do something they will lose their status as "smart."

Kids with a growth mind-set, alternatively, tend to care about learning. Those who have been encouraged to focus on their efforts rather than on their intelligence see effort as a positive thing. It sparks their intelligence and causes it to grow. These students increase their efforts in the face of failure and look for new learning strategies rather than giving up. This is the epitome of resilience.

The Key to Lifelong Learning and Success

Growing research in psychology and neuroscience also supports the idea that a growth mind-set is the real catalyst for outstanding achievement. Studies of the brain show that our mind has much more plasticity over time than we ever dreamed. The basic facets of our intelligence can be improved through learning even into old age. It's persistence and dedication when faced with obstacles that are the key ingredients to overall success in a lot of areas.

This is really eye-opening. How many smart and talented people do you know who have never lived up to their potential because they had a fixed mind-set about being naturally smart—so they stopped trying when success didn't come easily?

Some interesting studies conducted on fifth-graders by Dweck and colleagues aimed to show how praise affects students' performance. Groups of students were given specific kinds of tasks to work on and then received different kinds of praise for their work. Some students heard things like "You must be smart at solving these problems" (encouraging a fixed mind-set) and others heard "You must have worked hard on solving these problems" (encouraging a growth mind-set). Afterward, the students were asked to agree or disagree with certain statements, such as "Your intelligence is something basic about you that you can't really change." The students who were praised for being smart agreed with these statements much more than the ones who were praised for their effort.

In a follow-up study, the students were asked to give their definition of intelligence. Those who had been praised for intelligence said they thought it was an innate trait that was fixed, whereas the ones who were praised for effort thought it was something you could develop with work.

Students were then given the option to work on an easy problem or a difficult one. The students who were praised for intelligence chose to do the easy problem rather than the hard one, presumably to ensure a perfect performance. The ones praised for effort chose the challenging one with the opportunity to learn. Afterward, all the students were given a complicated task to work on. The children with the fixed mind-set lost their confidence and enjoyment the minute they had difficulties solving the problem. For them, success meant being innately smart, so struggling meant they were not. The kids with growth mind-sets, on the other hand, didn't lose their confidence and were eager to try to solve the problem.

When the task was made easier again, the students praised for their intelligence had already lost their confidence and motivation from the harder problem and did poorly overall. As a group, they did worse on the same kind of task they had been given in the beginning, while the group praised for effort continually improved and did an excellent job overall.

Perhaps what was most interesting, though, was when asked anonymously to report their scores, the fixed mind-sets overreported their results more than 40 percent of the time. Their self-image was so tied up in their scores that they were reluctant to admit failure, whereas the growth mind-sets adjusted their scores upward 10 percent of the time. Studies conducted on cheating in schools confirm that students today are far more likely to cheat in order to get high grades than in previous generations, a reflection of increased pressure to achieve coupled, in many cases, with a fixed mind-set.

We think telling kids how smart they are boosts their confidence, but in the face of difficulty, it actually makes them *lose* confidence! Praising students for their intelligence doesn't give them the motivation or resilience crucial to being successful, but can instead give them a fixed mind-set full of vulnerability. In contrast, effort or "process" praise—praise for engagement, perseverance, strategies, improvement, and so on—fosters motivation and resilience. It highlights for kids what they've done to be successful and what they need to do to be successful in the future.

Interestingly, a recent *New York Times* article reports that even businesses nowadays are looking for people with a growth mind-set rather than a fixed mind-set. Since people with a growth mind-set are better at fostering teamwork and resolving challenges without getting stressed, they are much more attractive to most organizations. The innately talented, or the fixed mind-sets, are more egocentric and concerned about being the biggest star in the organization. It's the ones who can tackle a task with perseverance and resilience, incorporating colleagues with gratitude, who will ultimately get the sought-after position—and even make it to CEO status.

Some examples of process praise:

"I like the way you tried putting the puzzle pieces together again and again. You didn't give up and you found a way to put it together!"

"You practiced that dance so many times and the effort really showed today! You danced really well!"

"I am so proud of you for how you shared your snack with your brother. It makes me so happy to see you sharing."

"It was a long, difficult assignment, but you stayed at it and got it done. I am so proud of you for how you stayed focused and kept working. Well done!"

Tips for Authenticity

1. Root out self-deception

Be honest with yourself first and foremost. Learn how to look at your own life authentically. Being able to detect and define your own emotions and how you truly feel is a huge milestone. Teaching emotional honesty to your kids and preventing them from becoming self-deceptive is a great gift. Listening to and expressing one's own true thoughts and feelings is what keeps us on the right track to going after what makes us happy in life. Being honest with ourselves is how we calibrate our internal compasses to set ourselves in the right direction.

2. Answer with honesty

If your kids ask a question, give them an honest answer. Of course, your answer has to be age appropriate and commensurate with their level of understanding. Being sincere in your responses is important in all aspects of life, even the difficult ones. By not being authentic, you undermine your child's ability to sense what is true and false. Kids are incredible lie detectors, and they can feel unstable if you are being fake.

3. Use examples from your own childhood

Whether it's the doctor's office or a difficult situation or just a fun time, kids like to hear about your experiences and how you felt when you were little, particularly when it's true and heartfelt. This gives them a better understanding of who you are and lets them know that their situation is normal even if they are scared, happy, or sad.

4. Teach honesty

Talk with your children about how important honesty is in your family. Make it a value. Let them know you put more emphasis on honesty than on the punishment for bad behavior. If you confront your kids accusingly with anger or threats and are punitive when they misbehave, they might become afraid to tell the truth. If you make it safe for them, they will be honest. Remember, it takes a lot to confess or tell the truth for anyone at any age. It doesn't always come naturally. It's up to us to teach them to be courageous enough to be honest and vulnerable and confess when necessary. Be nonjudgmental. This kind of honest relationship, if fostered well, will be paramount during the teenage years.

5. Read stories that encompass all emotions

Read all kinds of stories to your child. Don't be afraid if they don't all have happy endings. Actively choose stories that have difficult topics too, and stories that don't conclude in a "storybook" way. Children learn a lot from sadness and tragedy (being age appropriate, of course), and they open up honest communication between you about different aspects of life that are just as important as the prince getting the princess. Being exposed to peaks and valleys of life encourages empathy, resilience, and feelings of meaningfulness and gratitude for our own lives.

6. Use process praise

Remember that the most meaningful and useful praise is based on quality, not quantity. Keep the praise focused on the process or effort children put in rather than on innate abilities: "You studied hard for your test, and your improvement shows it. You went over the material many times, made cue cards, and quizzed yourself. That really worked!"

Try to come up with some more examples of process praise. Practice makes perfect—the more you try to use process praise, the better you will get at it. See if you can avoid saying, "You are so smart." By focusing on the effort involved, you will give your children the tools to understand that it is the perseverance, not the innate ability, that matters most. In the long run, they will have stronger self-esteem because of it.

7. Don't use praise as a default response

Don't overuse praise for things that are too easy. This can teach your child that he is only praiseworthy when he completes a task quickly, easily, and perfectly, and that does not help him embrace challenges. If, for example, a child gets an A easily without much effort, try saying, "Well that was way too easy for you!

Why don't we try doing something more challenging that you can learn from?" The goal is not to make easily performed tasks the basis for our admiration.

8. Focus on effort—and keep it genuine

Be careful praising for failures or mistakes. Saying things like "Well done!" "You did your best!" "Better luck next time!" can be heard as pity. Focus on what they did accomplish and how it can be worked on—"I know you missed the goal, but it was very close! Let's get out and practice next week so you'll get it next time! Remember, practice is the key!" By focusing on the effort involved in learning, we create a growth mind-set. This mind-set is helpful in all aspects of life, from work to relationships.

9. Teach children not to compare themselves with others

They need to realize themselves whether they did their best on a project or if they feel they can do more. Not everyone can be the best at everything, but you can be the best for yourself. This focus, as opposed to competing with others, fosters well-being.

10. Highlight your unique and authentic perspective, and your child's, by saying "for me"

Try adding "for me" after a sentence to emphasize your understanding that your experience of a given situation isn't necessarily the same as your child's. For example, if you have an argument with your child about food being too hot, it is important to remember that although it isn't too hot for you, it may be too hot for her. Saying, "The food isn't too hot for me," lets her know that you understand this. Or instead of saying, "The weather isn't cold," you could say, "The weather isn't cold for me." This respect for individual experience builds trust and respect—and helps kids recognize and honor their own experience.

CHAPTER 4

R Is for Reframing

"It's snowing still," said Eeyore gloomily.
"So it is."
"And freezing."
"Is it?"
"Yes," said Eeyore. "However," he said, brightening up a little, "we haven't had an earthquake lately."

A. A. MILNE, *WINNIE-THE-POOH*

As an American married to a Dane, Jessica remembers the first time she realized that her husband was doing something differently with their children than she was. Whenever there was a negative situation of some kind, she tended to respond a little too quickly. With exasperation, she would throw up her hands. "She won't do it! She never listens!" Her husband, meanwhile, always had more patience, more calm, and a magical sentence on hand for each situation that could amaze even Jessica. It was like a window opening up into a darkened room, shedding new light on a discussion she had previously seen no possibility in. He could put something unpleasant in a more positive light. He could make a black-and-white situation seem a little more gray. Pain became less painful and anger more tempered. Jessica noticed his family and friends doing the same with their children. Where was this magical phrase book these Danes were using?

One morning, listening to her husband delicately alter their daughter's language around her fear of spiders, it hit Jessica just how powerful this influence was going to be for her daughter's future. As she watched her daughter carefully study the spider with him and marvel at it instead of screaming in fear and saying, "Eew!" it struck her that the "Danish way" of using language was hugely important. Because it wasn't just about the language; it was about using the language to create a perception shift.

Taking Off Your Old Glasses (Again)

You see, the way we view life and filter our day-to-day experiences affects the way we feel in general. Many of us are unaware that how we see things is an unconscious choice. We feel that our perception of life is the truth. It's our truth. We don't think of our perception as a learned way of seeing things (often picked up from our parents and our culture). We see it as just the way things are. This set way of "the way things are" is called a "frame," and this frame through which we see the world is our perception. And what we perceive as the truth feels like the truth.

What if we could see the truth in a new way?

But what if we could see the truth in a new way? What if we could take the truth as we see it and put it into a new mental frame—a broader, more open-minded frame—and hang it back on the wall? If we looked at that picture we call "the truth" again, how would we see it?

Imagine you're standing in an art gallery. The picture is

hanging on the wall and there is a guide who is pointing out its subtle details to you. You begin to notice things you didn't see before. These new details you see were clearly there before, but you missed them because you were too focused on what you thought was the most obvious theme. It was a negative picture, you concluded. The man was mean, the woman was helpless, and the mood was somber. You are about to move on, but now you realize, with the help of the guide, that there is an entirely different story line to focus on in the picture. You now see that there are jovial people bearing gifts arriving in the window behind the couple. The man is being bitten by a dog, which is why he looks mean, and the woman is being helpful, not helpless. There is a child laughing in the background you hadn't noticed, and the light streaming through the window is extraordinary. In the very same picture, there are many other things to focus on that you hadn't even seen. It feels exhilarating to experience this mental shift and discovery. Your memory of that picture will now be completely different, and the way you share your observations about it with others will be too. With practice, finding these alternative story lines becomes a skill, not a struggle. And the guide pointing out these alternate story lines in the future will be you.

Realistic Optimism

Do you think the ability to reframe a stressful situation—a family issue, a coworker problem, a disobedient child—like you did with this picture could actually change your well-being? The answer is a resounding yes! And it's something the Danes have been doing for centuries. They teach their children this invaluable skill, and learning how to reframe early helps them grow up to be naturally better at it as adults. And being a master reframer is a cornerstone of resilience.

Ask a Dane how he thinks the weather is when it is freezing, gray, and raining out, and he will unwittingly answer:

"Well, it's a good thing I am at work!"

"Glad I am not on holiday!"

"I am looking forward to cozying at home inside tonight with the family."

"There isn't bad weather, only bad clothing!"

Try to get a Dane to focus on something really negative in any kind of topic and you will be mystified at how she is able to find a more positive outlook on the conversation.

"Too bad it's the last weekend of vacation," you might say.

"Yes, but it's the first weekend of the rest of our lives!"

And we don't mean to say that Danes have an exaggerated positive outlook, using reframing to sugarcoat their lives.

They aren't floating around on a cloud of optimism often associated with super-happy people. The "Everything is so great and wonderful!" types. The ones who look like their smile is glued on and they are high on life all the time. No, Danes don't pretend that negativity doesn't exist. They just point out in a rather matter-of-fact way that another side also exists that you may never have even considered thinking about. They choose to focus on the good in people instead of on the bad. They change their expectations to focus on the bigger picture rather than getting trapped by one aspect of an argument, and they generally tend to be more tempered in their assumptions. Danes are what psychologists call "realistic optimists."

Realistic optimists are different from those overly optimistic people with the glued-on smiles—those people who sometimes appear to be fake because life sounds too perfect. The problem with being overly positive and optimistic is the same as at the opposite end of the spectrum, with people who are overly negative and pessimistic. Very negative people tend to ignore positive information, which can bring them down and prevent them from seeing a positive reality. Overly positive people, on the other hand, tend to ignore negative information, which can make them oblivious to important negative realities. It's risky to force yourself to believe that everything is great, saying, "No, there's no problem at all," when really there is. Underestimating negative situations has the potential to deliver a much bigger blow when you're hit with one. This is related to the self-deception we talked about in chapter 3. Being in touch with reality but focusing on the more positive angles is much more in line with being a realistic optimist.

Realistic optimists merely filter out *unnecessary* negative information. They learn to tune out negative words and occurrences and develop a habit of interpreting ambiguous situations in a more positive manner. They don't see things as only bad or good or black or white but instead realize that there are many shades in between. Focusing on the less negative aspects of situations and finding a middle ground reduces anxiety and increases well-being.

The Skill of Reframing

Numerous organizations in the U.S. are training their workers in the skill of reinterpreting information, or reframing, because it is seen as a key trait in resilience. In a *Harvard Business Review* article, Dean M. Becker, founder of Adaptiv Learning Systems, observes, "More than education, more than experience, more than training, a person's level of resilience will determine who succeeds and who fails. That's true in the cancer ward, it's true in the Olympics, and it's true in the boardroom." The ability to reframe negative situations is a key element to being resilient.

Numerous studies show that when we deliberately reinterpret an event to feel better about it, it decreases activity in areas of the brain involved in the processing of negative emotions and increases activity in areas of the brain involved in cognitive control and adaptive integration. In one reframing study, two groups of participants were shown pictures of angry faces. The first group was told to think the people in the pictures had just had a bad day and their faces had nothing to do with them. The other group was told to feel whatever emotions the faces elicited. What they found was that the group that had been trained to adjust their attitude about the angry faces weren't disturbed at all—in fact, recorded electrical brain activity

We feel what we think.

showed that the reframing had wiped out the negative signals in their brain—whereas the group that had been instructed to feel whatever came to mind were disturbed by the faces. We feel what we think.

In a study done by researchers at Stanford University, participants with phobias were exposed to spiders and snakes. One group was trained to reframe their experience, and the other wasn't. The trained group showed significantly less fear and panic than the control group, and they experienced lasting changes in emotional responses when they were later exposed again to the spiders and snakes. This demonstrates the durable effects of cognitive reframing.

So not only does reframing change our brain chemistry, but it helps how we interpret pain, fear, anxiety, and the like. And this reframing is directly related to the language we use—both out loud and in our head.

The Limitations of Limiting Language

Limiting language, on the other hand, has the opposite effect. Saying things like "I hate flying," "I am terrible at cooking," or "I have no willpower; that's why I am so fat" is limiting language. "I really enjoy traveling once I get off the plane," "I prefer using recipes when I cook," and "I am trying to eat healthy and walk more now" present completely different ways of looking at the same things. It's less black and white and less limiting, and it has a completely different feel. Our language is a choice, you see, and it's crucial because it forms the frame through which we see the world. By reframing what we say into something more supportive and less defining, we actually change the way we feel.

Where the Danish tendency to reframe comes from is unclear. Realistic optimism just seems to be a default setting in Denmark; these language choices associated with reframing are passed on through generations. Most Danes are unaware that they have this gift—it is so much a part of the way they are. And we are convinced it is one of the reasons Danes are constantly voted so happy.

How Reframing Works with Children

Reframing with children is about the adult helping the child to shift focus from what she thinks she can't do to what she can do. The adult helps the child see situations from different angles and gets her to focus on the less negative outcomes or conclusions. With practice, this can become a default setting—for both parent and child.

When you or your children use limiting language such as "I hate this," "I can't do it," "I am not good at that," and so on, you create a negative story line. The plot may have us convinced that we aren't good at anything or we are doing everything wrong. A child who is told limiting stories about "how he is" or how he should do or feel things in various situations, he begins to build coping strategies based on a distrust of his own abilities in the face of new challenges. "She isn't very good at sports"; "He is so messy"; "She is too sensitive." These are all very defining. The more of these statements children hear, the more negative conclusions about themselves they make.

To reduce the problem, it helps to find and create a different narrative for your children. Leading them to a new, broader, or more ambiguous picture about themselves and the world around them helps them to reframe. And this skill will transfer to how they learn to see and interpret life and others as well.

In Iben's practice as a narrative psychotherapist, she focuses a lot on reframing and, even more in-depth, on "reauthoring." She helps people look at the beliefs they have about themselves and the beliefs they put on their kids without realizing it. Statements such as "He is antisocial," "She isn't very academic," "He is terrible at math," and "She is so selfish" all become behavior your children try to make sense of and identify with. Children can hear parents say these things much more often than you realize. Soon, they believe that it must be how they are. When new behavior doesn't fit into this label, they don't even try to make sense of it because they have already identified themselves as being uncoordinated, shy, or terrible at math.

The language we use is extremely powerful. It is the frame through which we perceive and describe ourselves and our picture of the world. Allan Holmgren, a well-known Danish psychologist, believes that our reality is created in the language we use. All change involves a change in language. A problem is only a problem if it is referred to as a problem.

The Power of Labels

Many of these labels and story lines, you see, follow us into adulthood. So much of what we think about ourselves as adults comes from the labeling we were given as children—lazy, sensitive, selfish, stupid, smart. Think about it: What are your beliefs about who you are, and how many of them came from what you were told as a child? Many of us continue to live up to and compare ourselves with these labels unconsciously for the rest of our lives. By separating ourselves from these labels, we open up new paths of change for ourselves and our children.

Consider how common it is to hear people talking about kids having disorders these days, even if they have never even seen a psychologist. It seems like it has become completely natural to describe children, our own and others', as having psychological problems. Shyness is called Asperger's, kids who have lots of energy are labeled ADHD, children who don't constantly smile must be showing symptoms of depression, and the latest thing we heard was a quiet child who was described as having sensory processing disorder. The parents were worried, the daughter was worried, and it was worrying to think how labeling her like that, without a diagnosis or even a doctor's appointment, could affect her for the rest of her life.

Saying so nonchalantly that children have a psychological or neurological disorder as if they are hungry or cold is very serious. Not only does it belittle the severity and seriousness of those who truly suffer from these conditions, but it also labels children unfairly. When they hear a plotline repeated about their lives, they begin to associate themselves with these labels and draw identity conclusions from them. These narratives become their life story, and it is very hard to get out of them. So we are encouraging the very things we don't like in ourselves or in our children by saying them and then repeating them. By reframing, or reauthoring, we can help rewrite our own and our children's futures.

Reauthoring

Iben shares an example of how she helps adults and children with reauthoring in her practice. When someone comes to her who is unhappy with the way his life is going, she tries to talk about the things he says about himself. She'll talk with him about his negative identity conclusions and try to separate him from these labels. For example, one of her patients said that she was lazy and scatterbrained and that it was ruining her life. So Iben asked her about this and what kinds of feelings this label evoked. The woman said it made her feel awful, especially when she would forget something or get lost or sleep in late. These behaviors just enforced the bad feeling. Being lazy made her feel like a failure and that she had no willpower. Therefore, every time she said, "I am lazy and scatterbrained," she was unconsciously reiterating this plotline in her head to others and making it more prevalent in her life.

Iben then used externalization language, or language that separates the person from the problem. Laziness is not something in the genes; rather, it is something that can affect people at different times. Separating the person from the problem makes us more able to feel like active agents in our own lives to combat the problem.

Iben tried to help this client visualize laziness and describe it. Is it a dark cloud? Is it stifling you? What does it make you feel when it arises? The woman said it was like someone was holding her down. It was heavy air on top of her, and she was paralyzed; she couldn't turn off the alarm. It was foggy when she tried to read a map. It held her down when she wanted to exercise. It made her feel undependable, incapable, and pathetic.

They then moved on to talking about the opposite feelings of laziness. They talked about what she valued in herself. They talked about what she would like her life to be if she could shake off this heavy air that fell upon her.

They then drew on past experiences to find a different story about her life. It turned out that she had phenomenal communication and creativity skills. She was funny and a deeply loyal friend. She was very skilled in cooking and music, and she had plenty of experiences to pull from in which she hadn't been lazy at all. She and Iben talked at length about those experiences. So instead of focusing on the negative identity conclusion of being lazy and scatterbrained, they focused on the values and skills they wanted to "thicken" in her narrative. The more they focused on talking about the values and skills she liked about herself, the more positive and loving the story line about herself became. Slowly, she began to define herself in a new way.

She was now creative, strong, and dependable, and she felt she had the tools to reframe her perspective on her life and her identity conclusions even more. With practice, her outer voice became her inner voice. The problem was now simply the problem; it was no longer who she was—and it seemed unlikely that she would ever define herself as lazy and scatterbrained again. The power of that defining language was so much bigger than she had ever realized.

Thus, reframing or reauthoring isn't about eliminating negative events in our lives; rather, it is about placing less importance on them and focusing more on the aspects we do like. Just like in the painting from the beginning of the chapter: By being open to changing the frame, we can see a bigger picture and practice concentrating on other details that tell a different story. We can change our whole experience of life into something better. This is exactly the same for kids. We, as adults, are the guides to pointing out a more positive and loving story line for them too.

How to Limit Limiting Language

Saying things like "She is such a picky eater," "He hates reading," or "He never listens" is causing that behavior to define who children are. The reality is, every behavior has a feeling or a mood behind it. It isn't fixed. Maybe they are tired or hungry or upset about something. The more we can separate the behavior from the child, the more we can change how we see her and, thus, how she sees herself. This lets her know that she is OK and that the behavior is not her destiny. Labels, as we have seen, can become a self-fulfilling prophecy.

A stubborn child may be very difficult at times, but try to see the bigger picture and what led to that behavior. Instead of saying how impossible the child is and making him a problem, try noting the other sides of the story. Maybe the child who refuses to eat had a snack before dinner and really isn't very hungry. Maybe the child who won't get dressed is at the boundary-pushing age and doesn't understand why socks are important. And moreover, what are the other sides of that stubborn behavior? Perhaps the child is very persistent and decisive and shows great leadership skills. Persistence is a powerful characteristic that takes us far in life. Maybe the distracted child is very creative and really loves art.

By talking about and nurturing the positive aspects of an unpleasant behavior, we are helping our child focus on the better story line too. This also prevents a lot of power struggles and leads to happier parents and children.

The Danish Way of Reframing

Danes, on the whole, use less limiting language and don't tell children how they are or what they think they should do or feel in different situations. You don't hear a lot of adult opinions being placed on children. "You shouldn't be like that." "Don't cry." "You should be happy!" "He is mean!" "He shouldn't be like that." "You should tell him next time!"

They tend to focus more on using supporting language, which leads children to understand the reasons for their emotions and actions. If they are upset or angry, for example, they try to help a child become aware of why they feel that way rather than saying how they should or shouldn't be feeling.

"What's wrong?"

"Nothing."

"You look like something is wrong—is there?"

"Yeah."

"What's going on?"

"I don't know."

"Are you sad? Angry? Happy?"

"I am sad."

"Why do you feel sad?"

"I am sad because Gary took my doll at playtime."

"He took your doll. Why do you think he took your doll?"

"Because he is mean."

"You think he is mean? Is Gary always mean?"

"Yes."

"But last week you said you played a lot with Gary, right?"

"Yes."

"Was he mean then?"

"No."

"OK, so sometimes Gary is nice?"

"Yes. Sometimes he is nice."

Danish parents are good at helping their children conceptualize their emotions and then guiding them into finding something more constructive, instead of a disparaging or limited belief. This is the heart of reframing.

"So what happened when he took your doll?"

"I cried."

"So you were sad he took your doll. I can understand that. What do you think you could do differently next time if Gary takes your doll, so you won't be sad?"

"I can tell him to give it back. Or I can tell the teacher."

"I think telling him to give it back sounds like a good solution. Does Gary like to play with dolls?"

"Sometimes."

"Is there anything else you could do other than ask for it back?"

"Maybe we could play together with the dolls."

"That sounds like a great solution. We know Gary is actually a sweet boy, so next time you can ask if he wants to play dolls too."

"Yes!"

Finding the brighter side of things can be done with all kinds of situations, not only with people. With practice it becomes much easier to scan a scene and find the hidden details that reframe a situation into something more constructive. It can even be fun to do.

Once a child finds a better story line, try to repeat it so it sticks. But the solution should ultimately come from the child herself. This builds real self-esteem because she becomes the master of her own emotional responses. She isn't told how to feel and act.

If we hold on to the good in people, to separate actions from the person, we teach our children that we forgive them when they themselves misbehave. Imagine if we had said that what Gary did was ridiculous and mean. Children will remember that. When it's our own children who are doing something similar next time, they know that we judge. If we trust other people and know how to forgive, we teach our children that we also forgive them when they misbehave. If we maintain that it is human to fail, and that we can see other positive things despite that truth, our children will also be gentler on themselves when they fail.

Another way of reframing is to use humor. If you find yourself on the side of a soccer field and your child played badly and says so—"I played terribly"—a typical way of responding might be, "No, you didn't! You played great! The field was slippery! You'll win next time! You win some, you lose some!"

A Danish way of reframing with humor might be something like the following:

"I played terribly."

"Did you break your leg?"

"No, but I am a terrible player."

"But you didn't break your leg, did you? Are you sure?"
    (go down to check the leg) "Well, at least you didn't
    break your leg!"

"Ha ha, I am terrible at soccer. I should quit. I hate it."

"You hate it? Yes, you did play pretty badly today, but
    remember last week when you scored two goals?"

"Oh yeah, but . . ."

"Remember how you felt when you scored those goals?"

"Pretty good."

"I think I remember you dancing around the field and singing. Did you hate soccer then?"

"No."

"Exactly. So just remember how you felt last week, and let's think of what we can do to help you play better next time."

"Practice more, I guess."

"Yes, and let's go have pizza and celebrate the fact that you didn't break your leg!"

"Some days are bad; some are good."

Notice that in this example, the parent doesn't ignore the fact that the child played badly. The parent acknowledges it but uses humor to show how much worse the situation could be as well as lead the child to positive feelings he or she did have about playing soccer the week before. This is being a realistic optimist. You acknowledge reality, but you can still eliminate the unnecessary negative words and focus on the good feelings rather than the bad through humor or focus on another time of feeling good. If you choose to look at the positive aspects of any child's behavior, you are giving him the tools to deal with his uniqueness. It's all in the way you frame it. And practice makes perfect!

Tips for Reframing

1. Pay attention to your negativity

Practice noticing when you have a negative thought pattern. Just try to notice it and see how often you are using negativity to view a situation. Try to come up with different ways of looking at things that upset you, such as fears or worries, as an exercise. Try taking a step back in perspective and see if you can find understanding and another way to see things or a way to focus on a more positive aspect.

2. Practice reframing

Think about how realistic your thoughts are and try changing the phrasing. Consider the following sentences: "I never have time to exercise. I am so fat." "I am a terrible writer." "My mother-in-law is so annoying." Now try turning them into a different sentence. "I do manage to exercise at least once a week, and I am trying to eat salads for lunch, which feels good." "I am a pretty decent writer once I get in the zone." "I love my mother-in-law even if we have our differences. She is a great grandmother to the kids." It can be challenging to do, but we know it makes a difference in our brain chemistry, and this affects our well-being. At first it can even feel silly to do it, but the better you get at reframing, the better you will feel. Everything we see and say negatively about ourselves, our family, and our anxieties and fears passes directly on to our kids, so give the gift of reframing to yourself and your children and help them become better at coping with life's ups and downs.

3. Use less limiting language

Try to eliminate the black-and-white, limiting language. I hate this, I love that, I always, I never, I should, I shouldn't, I am like this, she is like that, and so on. Limiting language leaves little room to maneuver and is only viewing things from one's own angle. Try to use more tempered, less severe language. Use less judgment and more acceptance, and you will find yourself in fewer power struggles with your kids and your partner.

4. Try externalization language: Separate the actions from the person

Instead of saying "She is lazy" or "He is aggressive," try seeing these issues as external rather than innate. "She is affected by laziness" and "He is struck by moments of aggressivity" are very different from labeling them as "how they are."

5. Rewrite your child's narrative to be more loving

Make a list of your child's most negative qualities and behaviors, and write them out as a sentence. "She isn't very academic." "I think he has ADHD." "She is so stubborn." Then try to rewrite the sentences, identifying the source of those behaviors. For example, the one who isn't very academic may love reading and be extremely social. The one who has ADHD may be energetic and a fantastic drummer. The stubborn one may be a patient hard worker who doesn't give up. Try focusing on the positive side of your children's behavior so they feel appreciated for their uniqueness rather than labeled negatively. Rewrite the negative identity conclusions for yourself and your children, and separate the behavior from the child. This gives both parents and kids the ability to grow and rewrite more loving narratives about themselves.

6. Use supporting language

Help your children by using supporting language rather than limiting language. Ask questions to help them identify their emotions behind the actions. Help them identify their intentions and the intentions of others so they can understand how to lead themselves out of tough situations.

7. Use humor

Connect with your child and lighten the situation with humor, to help put things in a new perspective. But be careful not to negate the child's feelings or experience.

CHAPTER 5

E Is for Empathy

The best and most beautiful things in the world
cannot be seen or even touched. They must be
felt with the heart.

HELEN KELLER

For many years, Jessica and her sister had a very strained relationship. Being together usually involved a lot of eye rolling and feelings of annoyance. They didn't really like each other that much, frankly. Jessica thought her sister exaggerated her experience of their parents as kids, and her sister thought Jessica was spoiled and insensitive. Both of these attitudes caused them to be defensive and distrustful of the other, which led to tension, arguments, and growing distance, with little hope for ever repairing their fraught relationship.

It wasn't until Jessica saw her husband's relationship with his brother that she wondered if there was perhaps a better way. The two Danish brothers had just as many differences and issues as the two American sisters, but Jessica's husband always approached them with understanding and forgiveness rather than eye rolling and exasperation, and they had a very good relationship despite their differences. So one day it occurred to Jessica to try to really listen, without her preconceived filters up. She tried to truly understand how her sister felt and what she was angry about. And what she found was that as she listened to her sister like a friend and not like an embittered rival, the role she had fallen into, a profound shift began to take place.

Suddenly, Jessica really did see her sister's side. And she began to feel a genuine compassion for her—and vice versa. For the first time in their lives they were speaking to each other like true caring friends. Within a year the relationship had dramatically improved, and now they've grown incredibly close. Where once she thought they were doomed to become estranged, Jessica now depends on her like a sister should, and feels grateful to have her in her life. It's a positive sea change, brought about by practicing empathy together.

It's striking how many people are unfamiliar with the meaning of the word *empathy*. "Is that like sympathy? Apathy? Homeopathy? What exactly is empathy?" What's truly remarkable about this confusion is, if so few people know what *empathy* means, how many are incorporating it into their daily lives? Empathy is the ability to recognize and understand the feelings of others. It is the ability to feel what someone else feels—not only to feel *for* him but to feel *with* him. Simply put, it's walking a mile in someone else's shoes. And it's a lot easier said than done. Why is it so difficult? Does it have something to do with our culture?

A recent study has shown that empathy has dropped almost 50 percent in young people in the U.S. since the 1980s and 1990s, which is quite alarming. Meanwhile, the level of narcissism has increased twofold. Narcissism is an inflated view of the self, which tends to separate the self from others and to inhibit formation of meaningful relationships. The characteristics of narcissists are such that people focus on themselves so much that they lose focus on caring about other people's needs. There are many theories as to why this may be true, but no one seems to be completely sure about the reason.

The Narcissistic Personality Indicator (NPI) was developed in 1970 to assess narcissism, and many studies have demonstrated its validity. Jean Twenge and her colleagues analyzed NPI scores for college students between 1982 and 2007 and found that during that twenty-five-year period, the level of narcissism rose significantly and steadily. The level rose so dramatically that by 2007 nearly 70 percent of college students scored higher in narcissism than the average college student in 1982. What could be the cause of this?

The Heart of America: Survival of the Fittest

For many years in the United States, it has been believed that humans, like nature, are fundamentally selfish, aggressive, and competitive. This began with the industrial revolution. The structure of the market economy as well as the financial, legal, and political systems are at least partially based on this notion, which essentially pits people against one another. The "gospel of greed" on Wall Street is just one example that highlights this lack of empathy. For so long, evolutionary theorists, politicians, and the public have focused on competition and the ruthlessness of natural selection as the way humans are wired; it has essentially built the foundation for the individualism that defines being an American. Ayn Rand, the famous author whose work is admired by many politicians, champions the idea that human nature is fundamentally selfish and man is here for his own sake. Whether you believe in this notion or not on the surface, the reality is these beliefs are so ingrained in American culture that most people aren't even aware of it. It permeates everyday life. Competition and striving to be number one are part of what defines being American.

Let's think for a moment about the mothers you have met. How many truly open up and share what is going on with their kids? How many are really brave enough to be vulnerable and admit they aren't sure if they are doing things right? These days, it seems like fewer and fewer moms are able to show their vulnerability as more and more standards are added to the list of what it means to be a "good" mother— standards to live up to and, frankly, compete with other mothers over. Whether it's what you feed your child (breast milk, organic, sustainable, and so on), extracurricular activities (how many they are engaged in, and how successful they are at them), or education, there is often a sense of one-upmanship in what should be a simple everyday conversation. Of course, this sense of escalating competition isn't limited to mothering. It permeates all kinds of discourse. It can be very subtle, but if you pay attention, you may be surprised how often you notice it's just under the surface.

Many people feel afraid of really opening up and being

vulnerable because they don't want to be judged or rejected. And in this fear, many relationships get reduced to superficialities.

Our Fear of Vulnerability and the Discovery of the Social Brain

Brené Brown, a lead researcher in vulnerability, says that people are afraid to be vulnerable because they are actually afraid of disconnection. We so much want social connection that we become afraid to say something that might make another person reject us. And yet, being vulnerable and having empathy serve to bring us closer to each other. So we move from vulnerability to the other side of the spectrum, which is shame. Instead of trying to use empathy and understand why someone makes the choices she does (to breast-feed or not to breast-feed, to work or not to work—just to name a few of the big ones), we shame her. "How can she work and leave her child with strangers? I could never do that!" "How can she be a housewife? I could never do that!" "How can she breast-feed so long? It's disgusting!" "How can she not breast-feed? It's so selfish!" And so it goes on. The broad brush of judgment is swiped across someone else, and—poof!—all of your choices become superior and you are obviously a better parent, and that feels good. Because being the best is a value we treasure highly. The cruel irony is that we would feel a lot better to have a connected social network in which we could feel supported, not judged.

The problem with shaming and striving to be better all the time is that when our own feelings of vulnerability come up, we become very uncomfortable or anxious. And what do people do when they feel any kind of discomfort or anxiety? The most common reaction is to numb out. Food, TV, shopping, medicine, drugs, and alcohol are all good remedies for numbing things out and feeling like everything is OK for those moments. But it is only a Band-Aid. Yet everyone seems to have a box of these Band-Aids at their fingertips. In her TED talk on vulnerability, Brown says, "We are the most in-debt, obese, addicted, and medicated society in the world." It makes us ask the question: What if we tried a little more vulnerability and empathy instead of shaming others? What if we stopped aiming for a perfection that doesn't exist? What if we tried to be more connected?

What if we tried to be more connected?

Groundbreaking research in neuroscience has revealed what scientists are calling the "social brain." This is a brain region that lights up when we are engaged in social interactions. Matthew Lieberman, a social cognitive neuroscientist, writes: "This network comes on like a reflex and it directs us to think about other people's minds, their thoughts, feelings and goals. It promotes understanding and empathy, cooperation and consideration." Lieberman believes that we are wired not only for self-interest but also for the welfare of others.

The Surprise of the Prisoner's Dilemma

To test the theory that humans are wired for both self-interest and concern for others, Lieberman set up a neuroimaging study using functional magnetic resonance imaging (fMRI), which tracks blood flow to different parts of the brain, while people performed a psychological test called the "prisoner's dilemma."

In the prisoner's dilemma, there are two people and a reward of ten dollars to be split between them. How much each gets depends on whether the other decides to split things fairly or not. If both players choose to cooperate, each gets five dollars. If one cooperates but the other chooses to "defect," or not split things fairly, the cooperative player gets nothing and the defector gets all ten dollars. If both defect, each gets one dollar. The challenge is to decide what to do without knowing your partner's decision. It's safer to defect: You'll get at least a dollar and potentially ten. If you cooperate, you risk ending up with nothing if your partner defects.

The results showed that, contrary to what the researchers expected, the players chose to cooperate more often than making the selfish choice of defecting. Moreover, the fMRI results showed that activity in the ventral striatum (the brain's primary reward center) increased as long as both subjects cooperated. And this reward center was more sensitive to the total amount earned by *both* players rather than to one's own personal outcome. This means that people got more pleasure from the happiness of others than from their own happiness! What could explain this? The Danes have always had a fundamental belief that caring about others' happiness is crucial for their own happiness, and judging by these scientific results, they are onto something!

The Truth About Empathy

Historically, empathy was considered something that separated humans from animals. Most believed that animals and primates didn't exhibit empathy. But the famous primatologist Frans de Waal demonstrates in his book *The Age of Empathy* that empathy is, in fact, visible in all kinds of animals. There are research findings revealing empathy in mice, monkeys, apes, dolphins, elephants, and other animals, but the general public knows little about them. This is because so many of our governing policies have been based on the belief that nature is a "struggle for life" and that we ought to build our societies on competition and selfishness rather than the full spectrum of what it means to be human.

From an evolutionary standpoint, empathy is a valuable impulse that helped us survive in groups. Humans could not have survived without empathy and solidarity. Contrary to popular belief, most of us do care about the welfare of others. This impulse has just been lying dormant from lack of focus.

People used to think that babies were born without empathy. But that is simply not true. We are all wired for empathy; we just have to learn how to connect the wires to make it work.

Empathy sits in the brain's limbic system. This controls memory, emotions, and instinct. It is a complicated neurological system involving mirror neurons and the insula. What many don't realize is that we are biologically predisposed to connect to others. This is made possible through many neuronal systems that are embedded in the right hemisphere of the brain, the mirror neurons being an important aspect of this. The self is not an individual entity, you see, but a relational construct.

> We are all wired for empathy.

Daniel Siegel, a clinical professor of psychology at UCLA, says, "Empathy is not a luxury for human beings, it is a necessity. We survive not because we have claws and not because we have big fangs. We survive because we can communicate and collaborate."

Empathy facilitates our connection to others. It develops in infancy through the relationship with the attachment figure. A child first learns to tune in to his or her mother's emotions and moods, and later on to other people's. What the mother feels, the child will feel and mirror. This is why things such as eye contact, facial expressions, and tone of voice are so important in the beginning of life. It is the first way we feel trust and attachment and begin to learn empathy.

Moreover, babies will sometimes soothe other babies with pacifiers or a fluffy toy when they hear them cry. They respond to crying from others by becoming afraid or anxious, and some even start to cry when they hear it. They may not understand the reason for the crying, or the emotion behind it, but they will learn with time and experience.

Studies show that eighteen-month-old children will almost always try to help an adult who is visibly struggling with a task. If the adult is reaching for something, the toddler will try to hand it to him, or if the child sees the adult drop something accidentally, she will pick it up. On the other hand, if the same adult throws something to the ground forcefully, the toddler won't pick it up for him. She understands that the action was deliberate and the adult doesn't want it. Even before kids are taught to help or to be considerate—perhaps before they understand it's an obligation—children are less selfish than often presumed.

The Responsibility of Parents

Parents have a big responsibility because they are the primary example of empathy and must practice being empathic themselves. This can be done with their use of language and their behavior. Children are constantly focused on their parents and will mirror them. Therefore, what they experience in the home will be crucial for their empathy development.

The kinds of families that can quash a child's ability to empathize are the families in which children are exposed to physical, psychological, or sexual abuse. Their healthy boundaries are breached, along with their ability to feel for others.

Any child who has suffered an attachment trauma will have his or her capacity for empathy damaged.

Other types of families that can affect a child's empathy development are the very overprotective ones. These are the parents who are afraid to let their children fail or feel the big emotions and who do everything to avoid conflict and fulfill their child's every wish. These parents sometimes hide their logical, irrational, and emotional reactions to "protect" their children. This hinders the children's ability to read others' emotions (because what they see and feel is not what the parents confirm), which in turn can reduce their capacity for empathy. Children from overprotective families are often the ones who grow up more prone to narcissism, anxiety, and depression. They aren't allowed to self-regulate because of the mismatch between feeling and action.

Children who are consistently told how to feel and behave will not develop in the same way as those who are acknowledged and allowed to express their full range of emotions. They may become disconnected from how they truly feel, which can make it hard to navigate life's many decisions in a healthy way. They may come to feel a lingering emptiness and dissatisfaction. How can we know what we want when we don't know what we feel?

Fostering empathy in children early on helps them create better, more caring relationships in the future. And we know it's these caring relationships that are the foundation for true happiness and well-being.

How Do the Danes Learn to Be So Empathic?

In the Danish school system, there is a mandatory national program implemented as early as preschool called Step by Step. The children are shown pictures of kids each exhibiting a different emotion: sadness, fear, anger, frustration, happiness, and so on. The kids talk about these cards and put into words what the child is sensing, learning to conceptualize their own and others' feelings. They learn empathy, problem solving, self-control, and how to read facial expressions. An essential part of the program is that the facilitators and children aren't judgmental of the emotions they see. Instead, they simply recognize and respect them.

Another program, which is increasingly popular, is called CAT-kit. This program is used to improve emotional awareness and empathy and focuses on how to articulate experiences, thoughts, feelings, and senses. Tools in the CAT-kit include picture cards of faces, measuring sticks to gauge intensity of emotions, and pictures of the body, on which participants can draw the physical aspects and location of emotions. There is also a tool called My Circle, on which children draw their friends, family members, professionals, and strangers in different parts of the circle to help work on understanding others.

The Mary Foundation has had a major impact on empathy training in schools as well. Mary, the crown princess and soon-to-be queen of Denmark, has created an antibullying program, which has been implemented across the country. Free of Bullying is a program in which three- to eight-year-olds talk about bullying and teasing so they can learn to become more caring toward each other. It has yielded positive results, and more than 98 percent of teachers say they would recommend it to other institutions.

Another less obvious example of empathy training in Danish schools is in how they mix children of different strengths and weaknesses together. Students who are stronger academically are taught alongside those who are less strong; shier kids with more gregarious ones; and so on. This is done subtly. The teacher gets to know the students with time and then seats them accordingly. The goal is for the students to see that everyone has positive qualities and to try to help each other reach the next level. The math whiz may be terrible at soccer, and vice versa. This system fosters collaboration, teamwork, and respect.

Studies show that there is a huge learning curve in teaching others. Students who teach others work harder to understand the material, recall it more precisely, and use it more effectively. But they also have to try to understand the perspective of other students in order to help them where they are having trouble. The ability to explain complicated subject matter to another student is not an easy task, but it is an invaluable life skill.

And as Iben witnessed firsthand during her years as a teacher, this type of collaboration and empathy also delivers a deep level of satisfaction and happiness to kids. This comes back to the social brain and what we saw from the fMRI results in the prisoner's dilemma. Contrary to what we might think, people's brains actually register more satisfaction from cooperating than from winning alone.

Perhaps, then, it is no surprise that empathy is one of the single most important factors in making successful leaders, entrepreneurs, managers, and businesses. It reduces bullying, increases our capacity to forgive, and greatly improves relationships and social connectedness. Empathy enhances the quality of meaningful relationships, which we know is one of the most important factors in our sense of well-being. Empathic teenagers are shown to be more successful because they are more purpose driven than their more narcissistic counterparts. And if you think about it, it all makes sense. Successful people don't operate alone; each of us needs the support of others in order to achieve positive results in our lives.

Maybe by focusing on actively teaching empathy to our children as they do in Denmark, we will make happier adults in the future.

The Power of Words

Knud Ejler Løgstrup, a famous Danish philosopher and theologian who has had a big influence on Danish thought, believed that parents have a responsibility to nourish their children's minds with more than just entertainment and the transfer of knowledge. They should also nourish their ability to empathize. He said that the words we use, or the stories we tell about others, are essential for teaching our children how to be able to put themselves in someone else's shoes.

When Danes talk about other children in front of their own kids, for example, it is quite extraordinary to hear the words they use. They don't actively think about them. They are simply stock phrases that all parents use to fill space when talking with others. But what is powerful is their tendency to point out the good character qualities in other children. It is very common to hear "He is such a sweet boy, isn't he?" "She is very kind, don't you think?" "That was very helpful of him, didn't you think so?" "He is nice. Do you think so?"

What is remarkable about this is to think how these word choices are laying the groundwork for seeing the good in others as a default setting in the future. By pointing out the good in others, it becomes natural to *see* the good in others. It becomes more natural to trust. It is rare indeed to hear a Danish person talking negatively about another child in front of their children.

What they do instead is try to explain the behavior of others and why they might have acted in an unpleasant way. "She was probably very tired and missed her nap." "Do you think he was hungry? You know how grumpy we can be when we are hungry." They try to lead their children to seeing a child's behavior as merely affected by a circumstance rather than labeling that child as mean, selfish, or obnoxious. This is the supporting language we talked about in chapter 4.

And, in fact, this is really how the ability of reframing

begins. Being able to easily imagine that someone might be having a hard time makes us much more able to see his or her behavior in an understanding light. Instead of swiping a broad brush of a negative label, we can lighten our perspective with empathy. This also makes us feel better because it saves a lot of time that would otherwise be wasted on negative energy.

Løgstrup wasn't being naive to think that trusting in others would always be rewarded. He merely believed that trust, like other "sovereign expressions of life" such as speech openness, love, and compassion, is a fundamental part of being human. "To show confidence and trust in others is to deliver oneself." And it's true. Trusting is very freeing.

The Danish Way of Teaching Empathy

One of the first things to consider in terms of teaching empathy is to distinguish between the capacity for empathy and the consequences—that is, how one should put empathy into action in relation to others. This must be learned, and it takes a long time and a lot of good examples from parents and others who are with children on a daily basis.

Let us give you an example. Lisa is playing by the sea with a shovel and Mark, a younger child, wants to play with it, but Lisa refuses. Mark starts crying. What should Lisa do? What many parents would do is give the shovel to Mark because he is crying. But what does this teach? Is it true that we have to always give someone what they want simply because they want it? This is, again, teaching how to do things because there is an extrinsic consequence rather than an internal rationalizing. Lisa plays with the shovel and can sense Mark is getting upset. She needs an adult to help her balance her own needs and limits and then make a decision that she can vouch for and take responsibility for herself. What often happens in these kinds of conflicts is the adults will have compassion for Mark and demand that Lisa carry out the adult's compassion, forcing her to give Mark the shovel. This is neither fair nor empathic. This doesn't mean that Lisa shouldn't learn to take into account others' feelings—not at all—but what is important is to teach children that parents have empathy and compassion for them as well, understanding how they feel and what their needs are, which will give them the tools to truly use it themselves. It also teaches Mark that he does not necessarily achieve anything by crying.

So what can Lisa's parent do? After letting the children try to find a solution themselves, Lisa's mother or father might read her body language and ask her if she wants to share. Perhaps the parent can suggest a deal—Lisa plays with the toy for five more minutes, and then Mark can borrow it, while Lisa starts a new activity. Sharing and playing together is fun—if you're in the mood for it. It's OK to say no sometimes, while learning how to share, and enjoy it, is essential too.

In the long term, these kinds of lessons in empathy can be huge. When you teach a child that she won't be forced to do something simply to appease another or just to make things easier, it becomes a powerful lesson in the long run. Teenagers who are exposed to the wrong kind of peer pressure will have an easier time standing up for what they feel is right if they have been shown that their feelings are valid from early on. If we raise our kids with empathy, they will have a much easier time understanding and practicing it themselves. When their internal compass is strong, it leads them in the right direction.

Another way that Danish parents foster empathy is by pointing out to their children the emotions of others. It's not uncommon to hear things like:

"Aw, can you see Victor is crying? Why do you think he is crying?"

"She looks angry. Why do you think she is angry?"

"I can see you are upset. Can you try to tell me why?"

It's very rare to hear anyone responding with:

"Don't be like that. There is no reason to be angry."

"Why is she angry? That is ridiculous!"

"You have nothing to cry about—stop crying!"

"Why are you so upset?!"

"You should be happy!"

Danish parents tend to at least acknowledge the emotion before discussing it with the child—"Oh? Why are you crying?"—and they get down on their level to show them they see them.

> "I see you are upset. What are you upset about? . . . Because she took your toy? She is just a little baby. I don't think she did it on purpose, do you?"

There aren't always good reasons for a child's emotions, or easy solutions for them, but by at least acknowledging them and trying not to judge them, we are teaching respect. Imagine if adults' emotional states were constantly disregarded as ridiculous, unnecessary, or wrong and we were told how to feel instead.

One of the pillars in the Danish way of teaching empathy is not judging. Danes try not to judge their children, their friends, their children's friends, or their family too harshly. All members of a family have a right to be heard and taken seriously, not just the one who screams the loudest. Being tolerant of yourself and others is paramount.

And remember, by fostering a more empathic, less shaming, and more vulnerable, authentic style in your household, you will be helping your children to grow up to be less judgmental of others—including of you—in the long run.

Tips for Empathy

1. ### Understand your own empathic style
   Some questions to ask and discuss are:
   - What does empathy mean for me?
   - What does empathy mean for my partner?
   - Where do we agree and disagree?
   - What are our values to the core?
   - How judgmental am I of myself and others? How judgmental is my partner of others?
   - How does our language style reflect this?
   - How can I change my language style to reflect a more empathic style with less judgment? Remember, this isn't easy, but with practice you will get better. Try listening to yourself first to see how much you talk about others, and then think of alternate ways to express yourself that involve more empathy. Remember, your children are mirroring you. Help your partner do the same.

2. ### Understand others
   Practice understanding others instead of shaming them. You will be amazed how often you are judging others and what a difference it makes to find a reason to defend them by putting yourself in their shoes. This is really putting empathy into practice.

3. ### Notice and attempt to identify emotions
   Help your child see others' emotions as well as ex-

periencing his own without imposing your judgment. "Sally was angry? Why was she angry? What happened? What do you think about what happened?" Not "She shouldn't have been angry and done that."

4. Read, read, read

Studies show that reading to children markedly increases their empathy levels. And not just reading nice books but reading books that encompass all emotions, including negative and uncomfortable ones. Dealing with reality, even at the level kids can handle, is honest and authentic and is proven to significantly improve empathy.

5. Improve meaningful relationships

Try using empathy to patch up some of your own relationships. Having fractured relationships has been proven to cause physical and psychological damage. Empathy and forgiveness activate the same region of the brain, which means the more you hone your empathy skills, the easier it is to forgive and be forgiven. Meaningful friend and family relationships are the most important factors determining true happiness, well above having a lot of money.

6. Be vulnerable

Try to be a better listener and don't be afraid to be vulnerable. It's the most connecting thing we can do.

Listen, be curious, mirror, and use metaphors to provide caring responses.

7. Seek out empathy in others

Surround yourself with friends and family who want to practice empathy and kindness. New mothers and parents are the ones who can benefit enormously from this support.

CHAPTER 6

N Is for No Ultimatums

It is better to conquer yourself than to win a thousand battles.

BUDDHA

We have all been there. We are tired, our kids are disobeying or not listening, and despite our best efforts, they continue to misbehave or annoy us, and we snap. Some parents scream and yell, some people threaten with time-outs or to take something away, and some use physicality.

We have seen numerous friends and fellow parents yell at or spank their children. It often comes from the frustration of their child not listening to an ultimatum. The scene usually goes like this: "You'd better do that right now or else!" or "If you don't stop that right now, you're going to get it . . . I mean it!" "If I ask you one more time, that's it!" And once the ultimatum is out there and all resources are exhausted, the parents feel they have to follow through to regain control, and the result ends up in spanking, screaming, or physicality of some sort.

Some studies suggest that up to 90 percent of Americans still use spanking as a form of discipline for their children. Jessica was spanked as a child, as was her sister. Parents who spank are generally just operating from their own default settings based on their upbringing, which is typically quite physical.

For many years, Jessica never questioned spanking as a way of disciplining. When she was in elementary school, corporal punishment by teachers had only recently been abolished. She thought it was completely normal and never felt she'd had a problem with it.

It wasn't until she was pregnant with her first child that she realized how different her husband's outlook on disciplining was from her own. Their discussions on the subject, and her growing understanding of her husband's Danish upbringing, led her to consider another way. The journey to this discovery, like so many aspects of understanding the Danish Way, was eye-opening.

Upon researching this book, we learned that there are currently nineteen states in the U.S. where corporal punishment is still allowed in schools. That is, hitting students with a paddle or a cane for misbehaving. Although corporal punishment in schools has been banned in thirty-one states, it is still allowed in private schools in all fifty states. This may or may not come as a surprise to you. The point is: Spanking is still prevalent.

In fact, a large-scale study conducted by the Centers for Disease Control and Prevention (CDC) viewing parenting practices across the U.S. confirms that we use physicality more than one might think. The study, which measured five different culture groups (Asian, Hispanic, African American, non-Hispanic whites, and American Indian) comprising 240 focus groups in six different cities, found that all of the groups claimed, at some time or another, to use physical punishment.

Even more striking were the differences across cultures in terms of when and where they spanked. African American mothers, for example, said they spanked right away. White and American Indian parents, on the other hand, were uncomfortable spanking in public. In a restaurant (a situation that came up often in the discussions), white parents often talked about taking the child into the bathroom for spanking, while American Indian parents preferred to delay it until they got home. This just illustrates that more spanking may be happening behind closed doors.

Four Parenting Styles

Beyond whether a parent uses corporal punishment or not, developmental psychologists categorize parenting styles into four distinct types.

Authoritarian: These parents are demanding and not responsive. They want obedience and have high standards—the classic tiger mom. Children of authoritarian parents tend to do well in school but sometimes suffer from low self-esteem, depression, and poor social skills.

Authoritative (not to be confused with authoritarian): These parents are demanding but responsive. They set high standards as well but are supportive in their discipline.

Children of authoritative parents are rated more socially and intellectually competent than those of other parents.

Permissive: These parents are highly responsive but seldom demand mature behavior from their child, depending instead on self-regulation from the child. Children of permissive parents tend to have problems in school and with their behavior in general.

Uninvolved: These parents are neither responsive nor demanding, but not to the point of being neglectful. Children of uninvolved parents do most poorly in all areas.

Authoritarian parents are described as being low in responsiveness and high in control. An authoritarian parental response to a child asking why would be "Because I said so." Children aren't encouraged to ask why; they are encouraged to do as they are told.

There are some challenges associated with authoritarian parenting. First, being very controlling can make kids rebel. Second, not offering much support apart from "Because I said so," "Pull up your socks," "Straighten up," and "It's my way or the highway" leaves kids on their own to regulate their emotions, which, when coupled with fear and shame, can be confusing and upsetting.

Authoritarian parents typically parent this way because

it's how they were raised and they feel they turned out fine. And maybe they did. But if someone says they smoked their whole life and turned out OK, does that mean smoking is good for us?

The Hard Truth About Spanking

A recent analysis covering two decades' worth of research on the long-term effects of physical punishment on children concluded that spanking not only doesn't work, but it can actually wreak havoc on kids' long-term development.

The study found that regardless of the age or the sample size of the children, not one of more than eighty studies succeeded in finding any positive association with physical punishment. Not one. What associations it did find were these: Children who are spanked may feel depressed and devalued. Their sense of self-worth can suffer. Harsh punishments can wind up backfiring because they can foster lying in children who are desperate to avoid being spanked. Physical punishment is linked to mental health problems later in life, including depression, anxiety, and drug and alcohol use. There's neuroimaging evidence that physical punishment may alter parts of the brain involved in performance on IQ tests and increase the likelihood of substance abuse. And there is data indicating that spanking can affect areas of the brain involved in emotion and stress regulation.

Parents spank because they think it is effective. And

maybe it is, in the short term. But beyond that, it becomes pretty ineffective. Kids learn to listen because they are afraid. Power struggles create distance and hostility instead of closeness and trust. Distance and hostility create resentment, resistance, and rebellion (or compliance, but with reduced self-esteem). And where do you go after hitting them if they continue the bad behavior? Hit them harder? Scream louder? Hit them some more? Not surprisingly, one of the most common long-term consequences of spanking is aggression.

Case in point: One mother in a spanking study conducted by parenting expert George Holden hit her toddler after the toddler either hit or kicked her, saying, "This is to help you remember not to hit your mother." "The irony is just amazing," says Holden. And let's not mention how many of us go on to repeat the habit unintentionally as parents. But do we ever ask the question, "Is incessant yelling or spanking really necessary?" The reality is that many of us don't ask that question until it is too late.

What are the world's happiest people's thoughts on spanking, screaming, and power struggles?

In Denmark, spanking became illegal in 1997. Most Danes think it is extremely strange, almost unthinkable, to use spanking as a form of disciplining a child. In Sweden, it was abolished earlier, in 1979. And now more than thirty-two countries, including much of Europe, Costa Rica, Israel, Tunisia, and Kenya, have similar laws.

The parenting style used in Denmark is very democratic. It is most closely related to the authoritative style. That is, they

establish rules and guidelines that their children are expected
to follow. However, they are very responsive to their children's
questions about the rules. Danes see children as in-
trinsically good and react to them accordingly. For
example, an interesting difference in language between Danish and English is what we call the toddler years. In English it is called the "terrible twos,"
whereas in Danish it is called *trodsalder* (the "bound-
ary age"); children pushing boundaries is normal

> Danes see
> children as
> intrinsically
> good.

and welcomed, not annoying and terrible. When you see it
that way, it is easier to welcome the misbehavior rather than
seeing it as bad and deserving of punishment.

As for screaming and shouting at their kids, you will rarely
hear this in Denmark. A household full of yelling is an extremely uncommon occurrence indeed. How do they do it?
One of the parents we interviewed summed it up pretty well:
"First and foremost, I think we must remain calm as parents
and try not to lose control of ourselves. For how can we expect
our kids to control themselves if we can't do it? That seems
unfair."

This doesn't mean the Danes are soft or weak—not at
all—but firmness and kindness can replace losing your temper
and going into immediate power struggles and ultimatums.
Avoiding these makes for a more peaceful and safer-feeling
atmosphere.

Parenting with Respect

The Danes want their children to be respectful, but respect goes both ways. You have to give it to receive it. Governing with fear is a problem because it doesn't foster respect; it fosters fear. There is a difference between firmness and fear. With fear, the child won't always know the real reason he shouldn't do something; he will merely want to avoid being hurt or yelled at. This doesn't facilitate a strong sense of core self. A strong sense of core self comes from questioning and understanding what rules are and why they exist, and then truly incorporating them and valuing them. Being afraid of something called a rule is very different. Living in a hostile environment of yelling doesn't help either. And likewise, you won't know if your child is being honest with you in the future if she is afraid of you. She may tell you what she thinks you want to hear out of fear. Fear is powerful but not conducive to an atmosphere of closeness and trust. You will have a much more positive influence and a genuinely closer relationship if you foster an atmosphere of respect and calmness in which there is no fear of blame, shame, or pain.

In fact, studies show that children from authoritative parents are more likely to become self-reliant, socially accepted, academically successful, and well behaved. They are less likely to report depression and anxiety, and less likely to engage in antisocial behavior such as delinquency and drug use. Research suggests that having even one authoritative parent can make a huge difference. These children are also more attuned to their parents and less influenced by their peers. In a study of American students, undergraduates were presented with a series of moral problems and asked how they would solve them. Students from authoritative families were more likely than others to say that their parents, not their peers, would influence their decisions.

How the Danes Practice No Ultimatums in School

One of the ways Danish schools promote democracy is by allowing students to create the rules together with their teacher every year. At the beginning of school, teachers talk with their students at length about what it means to have a good class and what values and behaviors they think they should implement to make it a good class. The rules can be anything from being on time to not interrupting to being respectful of others. But what is important is that everyone decides the code of conduct together. No set of rules for any class is the same. And they do this every year because the students are older and more mature and have different senses of responsibility than in the previous years.

The results are impressive. Iben recalls that in her daughter Julie's class one year, for example, if someone was being too loud or interrupting, the whole class had to stand up and walk around the room and clap their hands ten times. This was something they had all decided at the beginning of the year. So the kids who are being too loud feel a direct responsibility and effect on their peers, not just on the teacher. This can be a surprisingly powerful motivator to stop.

In Denmark, they devote a lot more time and energy to thinking of how to avoid problems rather than how to punish for them. Most Danish schools are supplied with different kinds of equipment to deal with various issues students may have. For instance, children who suffer from ADHD or hyper-activity can sit on an inflatable ball cushion, which helps them concentrate in class. This ball cushion has spiky massage knobs on one side. It stimulates the postural muscles so the student sits up straighter and keeps balance, which uncon-sciously increases attention.

Schools are also provided with "fidget sets" and "cuddle things" for kids who have a hard time sitting still, which can lead to disturbing others. Included in these sets are things such as stress balls and spaghetti-like strings they can busy their hands with, which helps them pay attention and focus. Kids who are really too full of energy or aggressive may be asked to run laps by themselves to help them burn off some of the ex-cess energy.

Danish teachers are also trained to follow a guiding prin-ciple called *differentiere*. This basically means that teachers learn to see each student as an individual with specific needs. They make goal plans together with every student and follow up on their growth twice a year. The objectives can be aca-demic, personal, and social. The idea is that by "differentiating" the students, the teacher is better able to understand their individual needs so he or she can act and react accordingly.

This is important because, as we have seen in the previous chapters, how you choose to see children makes a big difference in your reaction to them. If you see them as naughty and manipulative, you will react accordingly. If you see them as innocent and doing exactly what they are programmed to do, you are much more likely to react by nurturing and forgiving them, even helping them rather than punishing them. Patience is much more easily summoned when one sees the harmless intentions and goodness in an otherwise annoying child. This is a cycle that comes back to you. Good begets good. Calm begets calm. Remember, it isn't the child who is bad; it is the action that is bad. It is always important to make that distinction.

> Calm begets calm.

Avoiding Power Struggles

Iben recalls an example of how she avoided power struggles with a student when she was teaching. There was a boy in her class who was very provocative and rebellious. He was getting the label of "troublemaker." A lot of the students probably thought Iben was too easy on him, but she felt it was very important to stay away from framing him as a bad kid and having a lot of conflict with him. She knew he had a difficult home life, and she always saw him as a sweet, loving boy. He was funny and clever, and she focused on his strengths, choosing to ignore the rest so as not to reinforce the bad story line he had about himself. She spoke to him with respect and trusted in his ability to come out as a good person.

Many years later, the student came to a school reunion, despite having bad memories of the place. He had completely turned his life around and had come to say thank you. He remembered Iben telling him that she wasn't worried about him and that she knew he would do well in life. He said that the trust she'd had in him had given him the strength to trust in himself and become a better person. Iben was touched deeply. It was then that she realized how important separating the behavior from the person truly is. Trusting and helping people reframe themselves, and treating the behavior as the behavior and not as the child, help build a more loving story line of one's life.

So now we have seen why a more democratic approach is clearly beneficial for the well-being, happiness, and resilience of our children. How can we put the Danish way of no ultimatums into practice?

Put a Mirror Up to Yourself

Think of the things you most dislike hearing in yourself and then put a mirror up. That is what you will get from your child. If you don't like the yelling and the hands going up in exasperation, don't do it. If you don't like physicality, don't do it.

Stop Worrying About What Others Think

Stop worrying about what others think of you or your child's behavior. Yelling and physicality often get ratcheted up by the added stress of someone watching you. Whether you are at a friend's house or with your family or out in a restaurant or shop, keep your behavior in line with your values. It's about being authentic and behaving in accordance with what you believe. Don't worry about how others raise their kids or how your family thinks you should raise yours. Focus on doing what is right for your children, and believe in that success. Most parents simply repeat their own patterns. You are doing something much bigger and harder by making a change. Try forming a group of parents who share the same values as you within the Danish Way and support each other. Believe in your values and stand by what you are fighting for. The proof is in the pudding for raising happier, more resilient, and better-adjusted adults.

The Danish Way does work. If you feel torn about a power struggle over eating or being polite or belligerent in front of friends or family, don't go there. Breathe, remain calm, think. Use humor. Offer a way out. Don't worry how a friend might or might not judge you or your kids. Your kids, in the long run, will be happier and healthier, and that is what matters.

Chill Out and Remember the Big Lines

Know the difference between the battles and the war and don't take every battle. Is it really important that their clothes or hair look perfect all the time? Is it really important that they don't wear that Batman shirt one more day? Is it really important that they clean their plate right now because you said so? Or they try spinach because they need to right now? Is it really worth it? This is what you have to decipher and decide with your partner when the big lines need to be enforced. Maybe at a friend's house or in a restaurant isn't the right time. What are your big lines, and when do you really want to try to educate and enforce them? Ask yourself whether making a scene in public is being respectful to you and your child. You have to be consistent, but you don't have to raise soldiers. Remember, kids go through phases in which they don't want to do/eat/wear/say certain things. They grow out of them. If you are consistent with the big lines, they will understand them. The key is to have patience and the wherewithal to get through those phases without losing your cool and to stay focused on what is important.

Jessica's daughter refused to wear a jacket or socks for some time. It was very frustrating, and nothing worked except taking her outside with no jacket or socks, at which point her daughter realized, "Hey, I am cold; I should put that on!" It took some time, but she grew out of it. She didn't say hello to people for a while either. People stopped and said hello, and she looked away. Jessica kept reminding her, but she never forced it. One day, six months later, she started saying hello unprompted and continued to do so from there on in. Kids are testing things for themselves as well. If it becomes too much of a power game, everyone loses and life becomes more unpleasant than it needs to be. If you stay cool, so will they.

Examples of No Ultimatums: Offering a Way Out

The child is throwing something you don't want him to.

Typical response: "Don't throw that! If you throw that one more time, that's it!"

Take it away. Distract. Remove the child. Use humor. When you say no, be calm about it. Show the child what throwing it can do. Mime an "ow-ow" from being hit by the object and give it back. If he throws it again, show him again, shaking your head and looking distressed. "Ow, ow!" He may not get it the first time, but over time he will understand more and more.

Hitting or biting others is unacceptable, and in those cases, you should be firm and hold the child and tell her "No!" forcefully. Have her look at you and give you an apology sound and a caress so she learns the meaning of sorry and the nonuse of physicality early on. Remember, this needs to happen fast, because children forget in an instant what they did. You have to deal with that behavior directly in the moment. They may not understand the meaning of sorry in the beginning, but with time and learning to empathize they will.

Dinnertime Often Means Power Struggles

A child's reaction to food is often about how hungry he is. If he has eaten more in the afternoon, for example, then he is probably not very hungry. Or he may be so hungry that he needs to regulate his blood sugar to feel better. Eating to regulate blood sugar will surely affect how a child is acting. Using empathy will help you to understand where he is coming from and react accordingly. Being understanding rather than angry is a good place to start. Imagine how you would feel in either situation—if you were too hungry or full—and go from there.

Something to keep in mind: Teaching a child to enjoy and respect food is a great gift. Food is what sustains us, and having a healthy, loving relationship to it can create a lifetime of happiness. Check your own relationship to food and make sure it is as healthy as it can be. Mealtimes, ultimately, should be an enjoyable occasion for the family to come together.

Put a little of everything on your children's plates, and let them eat their food as they wish. Food situations should be nice and cozy above all, not marked by tension and focused on the fact that children have to eat. Most people would lose their appetite under those conditions!

If you make it a big deal, it will be a big deal. The food is there. If they want it, they can come back for it. We don't always love the food we are served or clean our plates or force ourselves to try things we don't like. Sometimes we do, but not always. Give children a way out when you can. They will have more respect for you when they discover a rule for themselves. Always keep in mind that you are the example.

Low stress makes everything uncharged, especially food. Remember, there are phases for your children with food as well. Giving healthy choices with food on the table, cutting out unhealthy snacks, and making mealtimes pleasurable rather than like a prison camp will teach your child that food is a lovely, enjoyable thing.

To encourage kids to eat, parents in Denmark often say, "You have to eat this food so you can be big and strong! Do you want to be big and strong?" The parent asks the child to flex her muscles to show how strong she is and assures her that it comes from the vegetables and healthy foods she is eating. It works more often than you might think!

Explain the Rules and Ask for Understanding

"Put your seat belt on."

"No, I don't want to."

"Do you remember why I told you to buckle your seat belt?"

"No."

"Because if we have an accident you could be very hurt and have to go to the hospital. Do you want to go to the hospital?"

"No."

(Put the seat belt on firmly.)

The more you explain things in ways that children can understand, the better. This approach conveys respect, and helps put you and your kids on the same side, sharing a common goal (in this case, going for a ride).

Getting Started

1. **Make an action plan.**
   What are your values with regard to your children? Include both your own and your partner's.

2. **Are you spanking or hitting?**
   Make a vow to stop. It isn't necessary, and it doesn't foster trust and respect.

3. **Are you yelling too much?**
   Make a vow to stop. Use it only when necessary. Yelling isn't pleasant for anyone. Your children mirror you; you are their role model. If you want them to

control themselves and behave, then you have to set the example of controlling yourself.

How can you avoid spanking and yelling? Find ways to reduce your own stress. Get more sleep. Breathe. Exercise more. Get some time away. Yelling and hitting often come from a lack of surplus time for yourself to process and have the space between your reactions to choose your response better.

If you feel close to exploding or yelling, take a deep breath. Go into another room and give yourself a time-out. If you can pass the baton to your partner, do it. Try to be aligned in your values of no hitting and yelling, and always form a strong front on what you do or don't want your kids to be doing. This alliance is crucial. It also helps because you can more easily keep each other in check on your outbursts. So if one of you is at your limit and ready to break, then calmly ask the other to take over. Within a short period of time, you will begin to see your children behaving more calmly as a result.

Tips for No Ultimatums

1. Remember to distinguish the behavior from the child

There isn't a bad child, just bad behavior. And there is also bad parenting.

2. Avoid power struggles

If you don't look for power struggles, you won't find them. Always think win-win, not "How can I win?"

3. Don't blame the child

Take responsibility for yourself, and try to do better next time.

4. Try to see that children are inherently good

Children are supposed to push boundaries and test the rules. They are not bad and manipulative. This is how they grow.

5. Teach your children

Guide them, nurture them, and educate them. Don't just punish them and see them as needing more discipline. Try finding ways to manage difficult behaviors. Don't label them as "sneaky" or "manipulative" or "terrible." Words matter. The behavior is the behavior; it's not the child.

6. Reframe

Find the better story line about your children and other people. Learning how to reframe and teaching your children to do it makes everyone more caring—and happier.

7. Remember: The cycle comes back to you

Good begets good. Bad begets bad. Out of control begets out of control—and calm begets calm.

8. Get your partner involved

Research shows that even one parent following the

authoritative (not authoritarian) style and keeping his
or her cool can make a big difference. But two is even
better!

9. **Check your ultimatums**

   Write down all the ultimatums you use on a regular
   basis. How are those comparable to the ones your
   parents used? How can you turn them into something
   more positive?

10. **Always think of your child's age**

    What can you expect from your child in relation to
    his or her age (zone of proximal development)? Every
    age has a "theme" of what can be expected from it.
    Children are not small adults.

11. **Be accepting of all kinds of feelings**

    Accept your child's feelings, whether she is in the
    mood you want her to be in or not. It doesn't matter
    what other people think of your child's mood. Every-
    one has a bad day sometimes, even kids. By not stress-
    ing over it, you draw less attention to it and you
    remain more respectful of her ability to self-regulate.

12. **Remember, protest is a response to something**

    Remember that protest is a way of communicating. It
    can also be a sign of growing independence. Appreci-
    ate it for what it is, instead of thinking of it as a terri-
    ble annoyance.

13. **Put the bad behavior in context**

Have there been any changes in your child's life that may be leading to behavioral change?

14. **Know what makes you snap**

It's important to know what your triggers are. Where is your breaking point, and what can you do to stop yourself when you get there? Do you need more sleep or some downtime or exercise? Listen to your needs and ask for help.

15. **Show that you listen**

Make sure you show your child that you listen to her. For example, when she asks for something, it is important to show her that she is heard and understood— even if it cannot be done. Repeat it so she knows that you heard her. "I can hear that you would like a lollipop, but . . ." Explain to your child why something can't be done. Teach respect, be respectful, and you will be more respected.

CHAPTER 7

T Is for Togetherness and Hygge

Good teams become great ones when the members trust each other enough to surrender the "me" for the "we."

PHIL JACKSON

When Jessica first met her husband's family and spent time with them in Denmark thirteen years ago, the experience was a little overwhelming, to say the least. *At hygge sig,* or *hygge* (pronounced "hooga"), which literally means "to cozy around together," was a way of life for them. Cozying around together involved lighting candles, playing games, eating nice meals, having cake and tea, and just generally being in each other's company in a cozy atmosphere. This very large family would come together for days on end just to cozy around without much of a break from each other. Jessica found this group gathering a little odd in the beginning, but after thirteen years of studying the phenomenon, we have finally worked out the secret to hygge.

Being American, Jessica's family was very different. They, as a rule, could only be around each other for limited amounts of time, after which they would need a break from each other. They did this respectfully but also knowing that taking breaks and doing their own thing was just a part of their way of life. Feeling the need to cozy around together for uninterrupted amounts of time would have almost seemed like an infringement on their individual rights as Americans. It also sounded like a recipe for disaster and arguments. In fact, she couldn't understand how the Danish families seemed able to cozy around together so long without more family drama. Surely, with siblings and relatives around, someone had to have problems, issues, or at the very least a neurotic tendency to gossip about. There seemed to be very little negativity and no complaining, and despite the number of people gathered, they operated together like a well-oiled machine. What in the world was going on?

Could this cozy togetherness time be part of the reason the Danes are so consistently voted the happiest people in the world? The answer is an absolute yes!

Research shows that one of the top predictors of well-being and happiness is quality time with friends and family. Our modern world doesn't always allow for this, but the Danish Way incorporates hygge into everyday life to guarantee it.

Hygge as a Way of Life

The word *hygge* dates back to the nineteenth century and is derived from the Germanic word *hyggja*, which means "to think or feel satisfied." It is a virtue, a point of pride, and a mood or state of mind. Hygge is something Danes identify with both in action and in being—it is part of their cultural foundation.

Because Danes see hygge as a way of life, they all try to make a cozy time together with family and friends happen. For example, at Christmas they work together to make sure there is maximum comfort. This is a team effort. It includes things like making the atmosphere warm with candles and good food, but it's also in their way of being. They try to help out so that one person or a few don't feel like the only ones doing all the work. Older children are encouraged to play with and help the younger ones. They try to engage in games that everyone can take part in, and they all make an effort to play—even if they don't particularly want to. Opting out of the game wouldn't be *hyggeligt*; it would be "not cozy." They try to leave their personal problems behind for those times and be positive and stay away from too much discord, because they value this cozy time together and want it to be just that. There are plenty of other times to worry about our lives and our stressors, and happiness comes from setting those times aside and being in the moment with the ones we love. For Danes, having a warm and lovely experience together is the ultimate end goal, and it is a great example to pass on to our children.

Feeling connected to others gives meaning and purpose to our lives, and this is why the Danes value hygge so highly. The individual is prized too, but without the interaction and support of others, none of us can be truly happy as a whole person.

> Feeling connected to others gives meaning and purpose to our lives.

The American Bedrock

This idea of togetherness, if you think about it, is quite different from the individualistic nature that forms a large piece of the American identity. The United States was built on the philosophy of self-reliance. We don't really need others if we are strong enough to succeed on our own. Why should we have to depend on support if we can do it ourselves? We glorify individual achievement and self-fulfillment with terms such as "the self-made man" and idolize the individual hero in all walks of life from political to social to sports. If you listen to sports, it is rarely about the team effort; rather, it's the individual who stands out: the famous quarterback or pitcher. It's the star who shines out from the rest. The people who help support that star often become blurred background noise. It's the hard work and the survival of the fittest we admire most. We are then raised to strive to be that star, to be that winner. Geert Hofstede, a world-renowned cultural psychologist, concluded in a very famous study about cultural differences that the U.S. has the highest level of individualism in the world. That is pretty incredible. We are so programmed to think about "I" that we probably don't even realize it.

This is not in any way saying that the U.S. doesn't have an incredibly strong community spirit. It is merely pointing out that, culturally speaking, we are more programmed to think individualistically. During a family gathering, for example, it is a lot more normal to think about how *I* feel than how *we* feel. We talk about things like *me* time or meeting *my* needs or figuring out how it makes *me* feel rather than how it makes *us* feel.

Moreover, it's fair to say that most of us would enjoy being a "winner." We would like our kids to be winners or at the very least to be the best at something and stand out. This is pretty normal. Who wouldn't want that? Just look at the number of awards given out in schools these days for any number of creative reasons. Whether it is for the silliest joke, the sweetest smile, or being the best jump roper in class, we all strive to win recognition for something. It's woven into the very fabric of our culture.

Alternatively, how many of us would naturally consider giving the winning trophy for "harmony of the group"? How many of us would gauge our child's success not on how well he played, but on how well he helped others play or how well the children played *together*?

When You Substitute "We" for "I," Even "Illness" Becomes "Wellness"

The concept of togetherness and hygge has many implications, but essentially it is putting yourself aside for the benefit of the whole. It is leaving the drama at the door and sacrificing your individual needs and desires to make a group gathering more pleasant. This is a much nicer experience to pass on to your children. They don't enjoy adult drama, negativity, and divisiveness. Kids are very happy to be together and cozy around! And if they learn to hygge, they will be able to pass it on to their kids someday too.

There is a famous fable about heaven and hell that we feel illustrates this concept well. In hell, there is a long table with a glorious feast of wine and food and candles, but the feeling is cold. The people around the table are pale and emaciated, and there is a cacophony of wails and cries filling the room. Instead of arms, they have very long sticks, which prevents them from getting the food to their mouths. Try as they might, it is futile. They are all starving despite the rich bounty of food in front of them.

In heaven, there is much the same scene. There is still the long table and the feast and the candles, but here the table is surrounded by jovial, laughing people. They are singing and eating. The atmosphere is warm and lively, and everyone is enjoying the food and the wine and the company. The irony is, they too have very long sticks for arms. But instead of trying to feed themselves, they are feeding each other. In this simple metaphor, a change in perspective—substituting "we" for "me" or "I"—has turned hell into heaven.

Teamwork in Denmark

In Denmark, from very early on, children work on group projects to encourage them to learn to help others and engage in teamwork and team building. Kids are taught to seek out oth-

ers' strengths and weaknesses and see how they can help people, going deeper than just what's on the surface. Danes also
encourage humility in their star pupils, so they
will be empathic and care about others. Only
caring about yourself isn't *hyggeligt*. In fact,
Danes are known worldwide for being easy to
work with and likable. This is because they are
excellent team players. They help others to help

> Only caring
> about yourself
> isn't *hyggeligt*.

themselves, and they are humble even when they are stars.
And who doesn't appreciate a humble star?

Social groups are also a big part of Danish life. Called
foreningsliv (or "association life"), these groups are based on a
shared hobby or interest. The objective can be economic, political, academic, or cultural. Their function can be to change
something in society, such as in a political association, or to
express themselves in a way that meets the members' social
needs, such as in a choral society or a bridge club. Statistics
show that 79 percent of Denmark's business leaders have been
active in associations before the age of thirty. Respectively, 94
percent, 92 percent, and 88 percent of managers with experience in associations believe that these years of involvement
benefited their social skills and interpersonal skills and gave
them a strong network. Ninety-nine percent of Denmark's
governors believe that participation in these voluntary associations promotes young people's professional skills.

This spirit of teamwork and cooperation is seen in all aspects of Danish life—from the classroom to the workplace to
family life. Seeing the family as a team fosters a deep sense of

belonging. Cooking together, cleaning up together, making time to enjoy each other's company—these are everyday ways Danish families foster a sense of well-being.

Singing and Hygge

An interesting way that Danes like to create hygge is in their affection for singing. From Christmas lunches to birthdays to baptisms and weddings, if there is a song-worthy event, they will most likely be singing.

The songs they sing are often specially written for an occasion, to be handed out and sung to a popular tune. These homemade lyrics are frequently hilarious, and everyone joins in discovering the words while singing together. Otherwise, the songs they sing come from a national songbook called "Højskolesangbogen." The Danish singing tradition dates back to the feasts of the nobility and aristocracy in the late Middle Ages, but over time it has been cultivated and is now more common than ever.

Nick Stewart, from Oxford Brookes University, has conducted research on choir singers and has found that not only does singing together make people happier, but it also makes them feel that they are part of a meaningful group. The synchronicity of moving and breathing while singing together creates a strong feeling of connectedness. Moreover, studies have found that groups of singers have actually been able to synchronize their heartbeats while singing. Performing together releases the "happy" hormone oxytocin, which lowers stress and increases feelings of trust and bonding. One only has to try group singing (once you stop feeling silly) to feel these powerful effects.

Social Ties and Stress Levels

The happiness level of the Danes isn't the only proof of the effectiveness of togetherness and *hyggelige* ties. Lots of research backs this up. Researchers at Brigham Young University and the University of North Carolina at Chapel Hill pooled data from 148 studies on health outcomes and their correlation to social relationships. When taken together, these studies, involving more than 300,000 men and women across the developed world, showed that people with poor social connections had on average 50 percent higher odds of dying earlier (about 7.5 years) than people with robust social ties. That difference in longevity is about as large as the mortality difference between smokers and nonsmokers. And it is larger than any health risks associated with many other well-known lifestyle factors such as lack of exercise and obesity.

In another famous experiment on health and social ties, Sheldon Cohen, of Carnegie Mellon University, exposed hundreds of healthy volunteers, who completed questionnaires detailing their social lives, to the common cold virus and then quarantined them for several days. The results showed that the quarantined participants with more social connections were less likely to develop a cold than the participants who were more isolated in their lives.

The immune systems of people with lots of friends simply worked better. They were better able to fight off the cold virus, often without any symptoms. Since stress hormones seem to have an effect on the immune response, it makes sense that a strong social life helps the immune system stay strong—it keeps physiological stress in check.

A research group in Chicago studied this effect and confirmed it. Social support does, in fact, help manage stress. If we know we have people we can talk to or turn to for help in difficult times, we are more ready to face life's challenges without breaking down. We are more resilient. Being vulnerable with someone helps lighten the load of the stress we're carrying. Many people strive to be stoic and keep things inside, but research shows that people who try to be tough in a tragedy will suffer for a much longer period than those who share their emotions and are vulnerable with others.

New Moms and the Danish Way of Togetherness

The calming effect of togetherness can particularly be seen in new mothers, who are under an incredible amount of stress adjusting to their new role. Lack of sleep combined with all the tasks in front of new parents can be overwhelming. Yet research shows that the reaction new mothers often have to this difficult period is to reduce the amount of social support rather than increase it. This is paradoxical because it actually makes the situation worse. Support from friends, family members, and parent groups has been clearly proven to help new mothers deal better with stress, thereby helping them see their children in a more positive light. This improves everyone's quality of life, particularly the growing child's. The more parents surround themselves with social support, the healthier and happier the baby will grow up to be.

In Denmark, when a woman gives birth a local midwife gets her details and contacts her within the first week to check in and see if she and the baby are OK. Even more essential is that the midwife also gives her the names and contact details of all the other women in her neighborhood who have just had babies too, with information on whether it's the first, second, or third baby, so that the women are well matched up. These women form groups and meet up once a week to share their experiences and provide support. The other mothers in the group also act as sponsors and will check in on a mother if she doesn't show up. They will call her or go to her house to make sure she is OK and has contact with others she can share with. These groups are a fundamental support during a very challenging time and an essential part of being a new mother in Denmark, helping both mothers and babies feel happy and secure.

The Danish Way of Hygge

We've talked a lot about social support, togetherness, and the importance of hygge. But here's a personal example from Jessica, about the moment she understood what it really is.

It was a sunny, fresh day. Jessica was lying in the hammock in her sister-in-law's backyard under a large plum tree with her husband; their young son and daughter were squeezed in between them. They were wrapped up like a swinging burrito, some with eyes open, some with eyes shut. Jessica pushed with one foot hanging lazily out of the hammock to keep them swaying back and forth. The wind was rustling the trees loudly; flickering rays of sun shone through the leaves in kaleidoscope patterns on their faces. It was a combination of touch, the sounds of warm nature, and the smell of her baby son's downy hair. She could feel his heartbeat, the warmth of her husband's leg next to hers. She was holding the foot of her daughter, who was cuddled up quietly with him. They were all there together.

"Ah, I see you are enjoying some family hygge over here," her sister-in-law said as she came to invite them in for lunch. And that, Jessica thought, after thirteen years with her husband, was hygge in a nutshell.

It's a feeling as well as a way of being. It is eliminating the confusion and hysteria of all else. It is choosing to enjoy the most important, meaningful moments of our lives—those with our children and family and friends—and respecting them as important. It is keeping them simple, making the atmosphere positive, and leaving our troubles behind. It is wanting to be there in those moments, choosing to be there, and helping contribute to having a cozy time. With a big family, this takes effort because like all team projects, it is working together toward a shared goal. This is the opposite of being an individual and standing out from the crowd. Everyone has to want it and respect it. Everyone plays a part. If we are all willing to contribute to creating a cozy time together, it dramatically improves family get-togethers, which in turn dramatically affects our well-being and happiness.

Tips for togetherness and hygge

1. Take the Hygge Oath

Make a pact with the whole family at the next gathering to think not about "I" but about being in the moment and trying to help make things run without conflict and controversy. You'll find the Hygge Oath at the end of this chapter, or print it out from thedanishway.com.

2. Be in the moment together

Everyone should agree to leave their daily stressors at the door. Don't focus on the bad things in your or someone else's life. Try not to dwell on negativity or speak negatively about others too much. Everyone must make an effort to be in that moment together. Keep it lively and jovial and non-accusatory. Kids mirror this behavior—and they feel safe and valued in doing so.

3. Practice "preframing"

Prepare yourself and your family for a get-together so that you'll get the most out of it without putting on your usual prescription glasses for the world or your family. Try to imagine what kind of experience you are about to have, and then think or talk about coping strategies that will help you remain calm while you are there. Remember that stress-free get-togethers with family greatly increase well-being. We are often stuck in our ways with different family members. Change it. Use empathy, reframing, and preframing to help.

4. Have fun together

When the whole family spends time together, play games, inside and out, that everyone can take part in. Put your personal preferences aside and simply get out there and have fun.

5. Make it cozy

Make the atmosphere cozy with warm lighting, homemade craft projects and decorations, and food and drinks you've prepared together.

6. Take a break from complaining

Whenever you feel the urge to complain, instead see where you can help out. This alone, if everyone agrees to do it, makes a huge difference in the level of happiness you'll share as a family.

7. Practice reframing if you get stressed

Reframing is truly a powerful tool. Everything can be reframed. The apple pie came out soggy? Now everyone can use a spoon! The soccer game got rained out? Time for a family Monopoly tournament! Remember, by doing this you pass it on to your kids, making them better at dealing with their own stressful reactions.

8. Keep things simple

We often have so many toys (both for adults and kids) that drown out the simple things, like the sound of the wind in the trees and the funny, sweet things our kids do on a daily basis. Distractions take away from hygge, which is about appreciating the most basic and real things. Keep it simple.

9. Stay present—and encourage your kids to stay present too

Use fewer toys, TVs, iPhones, and iPads. These should be avoided in gatherings so the kids, too, can be more present together. Play games instead.

10. Be connected

Try to learn and practice having a cozy time together. Learning to hygge together, your kids will pass it on, which makes for better family connectedness overall.

11. Encourage play

Invite the older children to play with the younger ones "in real life," not on an electronic device. Give them paints or let them play outside—just make sure family playtime is technology-free (or limited to certain times).

12. Encourage team building

Organize more team-building activities for children to encourage working together. Create scavenger hunts, build a fort, organize a tournament. Be creative.

13. Confide and share

When you are down or in a difficult moment, confide and share with your good friends and loved ones whom you trust. Remember, this reduces stress and helps you get over it faster. When the rough patch has passed, share with your kids, in simple terms, the story of how others helped you through.

14. Start a mothers' group

Seek out fellow moms in your neighborhood and build a support network. This type of support has been proven to be extremely beneficial, helping mothers cope with daily challenges and even see their kids in a better light.

15. Teach your children that the family is a team

Instead of "every man for himself," encourage everyone to root for the family team, and show your kids what part they can play—how they can help and contribute in various activities and projects. This spirit of cooperation and togetherness makes everyone feel more secure and happy.

17. Celebrate everyday togetherness

Remember that hygge isn't limited to big family gatherings. It can be achieved with just one or two people. You can declare a "hygge night," for instance, on a weekday, implementing the ideas discussed in this chapter.

18. Sing!

Sound silly? It works! It's fun and it's very *hyggeligt*. Why limit singing to the holidays? Kids absolutely love it, and adults do too.

Hygge Oath

———————————— • ————————————

*H*ygge is the uniquely Danish word for a special kind of to-getherness. Imagine that hygge is a space that your family can enter into. This special space will be *hyggeligere* (cozy) if everyone understands and makes an effort to follow the hygge rules. The hygge oath is something to discuss and think about in advance so that all participants who enter into the hygge space for a family dinner, a weekend barbecue, or a simple everyday family gathering will understand the "ground rules." When everyone knows that it's hygge time, they can each make an effort to foster closeness for the sake of the whole family. What follows is an example of a family hygge oath. Customize it for your own household—and let the togetherness begin.

> *We agree to spend "Sunday dinner" in hygge. We all promise to help one another as a team in creating a cozy atmosphere where everyone feels safe and no one needs to have their guard up.*

> *We agree to try to . . .*

Turn off the phones and the iPads.

———————

Leave our drama at the door. There are other times to focus on our problems. Hygge is about creating a safe place to relax with others and leave the everyday stressors outside.

Not complain unnecessarily.

Look for ways to help out so that no one person gets stuck doing all the work.

Light candles if we are inside.

Make a conscious effort to enjoy the food and the drinks.

Not bring up controversial topics like politics. Anything that creates a fight or an argument is not hyggeligt. We can have those discussions at other times.

Tell and retell funny, lovely, and uplifting stories about one another from the past.

Not brag too much. Bragging can be subtly divisive.

Not compete (think "we" not "me").

Not talk badly about others or focus on negativity.

Play games that the whole group can participate in.

Make a conscious effort to feel gratitude for the people around us who love us.

Where Do We Go
from Here?

———————— • ————————

And so the question arises again. After forty years of being voted the happiest people in the world, what is it that has kept the Danes at the top of the happiness charts for so long? As we have seen in *The Danish Way of Parenting*, it is, quite simply, the way they raise their children. It is a legacy that continues on, repeating itself through the generations, resulting in self-assured, confident, centered, happy, and resilient adults—and it can work for anyone.

As parents, it's important that we first examine our default settings, our natural inclinations as parents, so that we are better able to see where change is needed. Taking the time to see ourselves in the mirror, and see what we are repeating from our own family cycles, is the first step toward powerful change and powerful parenting.

Once we have identified our default settings, the principles of PARENT provide simple, effective tools for enhancing happiness in our kids and in ourselves.

Play helps children develop many essential life skills. Resilience, coping and negotiation skills, and self-control are just a few of the valuable lessons learned in un-structured play—as well as stress management, which lowers children's chances of struggling with anxiety as adults. Play helps develop an internal locus of control, giving kids confidence in their own capabilities, which powerfully lays the groundwork for happiness.

Authenticity helps children develop a strong internal compass because they learn to trust their emotions. Teaching honesty to ourselves and to our children fosters a strong character value. And remember that all emotions are OK. Furthermore, different types of praise affect children differently in terms of how they come to see themselves in the world. Giving empty praise or focusing too much on being smart can set kids up for feeling insecure and risk-averse. By engaging in process praise, we foster a growth mind-set rather than a fixed one, which contributes to a more persistent, deeply confident, and resilient individual.

Reframing is a powerful way to change our children's perceptions about life—and our own. How we choose to see things affects the way we feel things. Realistic optimists don't ignore negative information; rather, they simply focus on the other information at hand to write a richer, more loving story about themselves, their children, and life in general. Reframing can change our experience of the world, and it makes our own and our children's lives happier in the process.

Passing on the skill of reframing to our children may be one of the greatest gifts we can give, fostering future happiness for them and for following generations.

Empathy is an essential, and essentially human, tendency. While the level of empathy in our society has dropped and the level of narcissism has increased, research shows that we are wired more for empathy than for selfishness. By being less judgmental and shaming, we can better understand the vulnerability in ourselves and in others, which brings us closer together, forging deeper, more forgiving relationships and making us happier overall. Practicing empathy teaches children to respect others and themselves, which makes for a more profound sense of well-being.

No Ultimatums is a reminder that power struggles can lead us to lose our temper. Many parents scream or use physical punishment as a form of discipline. We lose control, and yet we expect our children not to. In an authoritarian parenting style, trust and closeness with their kids is replaced with fear. It works in the short term but can have consequences in the long run. The Danish, more diplomatic parenting style fosters trust and resilience in children. Kids who feel respected and understood, who in turn are helped to understand and respect rules, develop a much stronger sense of self-control and ultimately grow up to be happier, more emotionally stable adults.

Togetherness and Hygge are ways of fostering our closest relationships, which are one of the biggest predictors of a person's happiness. By learning how to hygge, or cozy around, we can improve our family get-togethers to make them more pleasant and memorable experiences for our kids. By leaving the "I" at the door and focusing on the "we," we can eliminate a lot of the unnecessary drama and negativity sometimes associated with family gatherings. Happy families and strong social support yield happier kids.

As we said earlier, you may already be familiar with some of the concepts in this book or you may not have even heard of them. You may already practice some of the Danish methods or you may practice none of them. We are convinced that if you take away even a few of the methods from this book and incorporate them into your life, you will be on the right track to raising happier kids. To find out more about the Danish Way, please visit thedanishway.com. There you will find tips, book suggestions, and more information on PARENT.

We believe that, together, parents and teachers can support each other in promoting the Danish Way to raise happier, more resilient kids. We all need support. By building a community together with the goal of practicing these tenets, we can cultivate some of the happiest people in the world in our own backyards. We hope you'll get on board and help us make it happen!

Special Thanks

———————————————— • ————————————————

Jessica Joelle Alexander

I'd like to thank my mom and dad for their unconditional love and for always believing in me. To my sister for her invaluable love and friendship. To my husband and his family for inspiring me to write *The Danish Way of Parenting* in the first place. And to our two wonderful children, the guiding lights of our life.

And to Iben, without whose contribution and expertise this book could not have come to fruition.

Iben Dissing Sandahl

First of all, I want to thank my husband for always loving and supporting me.

And a special thanks to my two beautiful daughters— without them I would not be the person I am today. I also want to thank my mother and father, who gave me life and have always supported me.

*   *   *

I am fortunate to be surrounded by intelligent and interesting friends and colleagues who listen, ask good questions, and inspire me.

And a special thanks to Jessica for being so brave as to take the initiative to write this book.

Notes

---•---

For those who want more information or facts about our sources and references, you can find inspiration here.

Introduction: What's the Secret to Danish Happiness?

OECD (Organisation for Economic Co-operation and Development) study. OECD Better Life Index measures the well-being of different countries. www.OECD.org.

The first *World Happiness Report* (http://www.earth.columbia.edu/articles/view/2960) was commissioned for the UN Conference on Happiness, held in April 2012. It drew international attention as a landmark first survey of the state of global happiness. The *World Happiness Report 2013* (http://unsdsn.org/resources/publications/world-happiness-report-2013/) found Denmark to have the happiest people. This is not the first time the Danes have been awarded this honor. Back in 1973, the European Commission set up a "Eurobarometer" to learn about the citizens of the European Union. Since then, member states have been surveyed about well-being and happiness. Denmark has topped the table every year since 1973!

"And the Happiest Place on Earth Is . . ." *60 Minutes* program, February 14, 2008. http://www.cbsnews.com/news/and-the-happiest-place-on-earth-is/.

"Women Around the World," Oprah.com, October 21, 2009, http://www.oprah.com/world/Inside-the-Lives-of-Women-Around-the-World.

Chapter 1: Recognizing Our Default Settings

Sara Harkness and Charles M. Super, "Themes and Variations: Parental Ethnotheories in Western Cultures," in *Parental Beliefs, Parenting, and Child Development in Cross-Cultural Perspective*, ed. K. Rubin and O. B. Chung (London: Psychology Press, 2013).

Antidepressant use went up 400 percent from 2005 to 2008. National Center for Health Statistics. http://www.cdc.gov/nchs/data/databriefs/db76.htm.

Attention deficit has become the go-to diagnosis, increasing by an average of 5.5 percent a year between 2003 and 2007. http://www.cdc.gov/ncbddd/adhd/data.html/.

Of children between ages three and seventeen, 5.9 million have been given diagnoses of attention deficit hyperactivity disorder. http://www.cdc.gov/nchs/fastats/adhd.htm.

As a parent, being aware of yourself and choosing your behavior is the first step toward powerful life change.

http://www.boernogunge.dk/internet/boernogunge.nsf/0/7F933F515B65A7B3C1256C64002D2029?opendocument.

Chapter 2: **P** Is for Play

"Remarkably, over the last 50 years, opportunities for children to play
freely have declined continuously and dramatically in the United
States and other developed nations, and that decline continues
with serious negative consequences for children's physical, mental and social development," says guest editor Peter Gray, a research professor of psychology at Boston College. http://www.bc
.edu/offices/pubaf/news/2011_jun-aug/petergray_freeplay
08252011.html.

Resilience and success: Gary Stix, "The Neuroscience of True Grit,"
Scientific American Mind, March 1, 2011.

The first actual pedagogy based on an educational theory was put
forth in 1871 by husband and wife Niels and Erna Juel-Hansen,
who, inspired by Friedrich Fröbel (1782–1852), created the first
Fröbel kindergarten. For the first time, play became important in
Denmark. Fröbel understood that children's play comes from
themselves. It is a natural expression of specific needs; therefore,
he highlighted play as a pedagogical method to promote children's development. Since then, there has been a strong flow of
free play in Denmark. http://www.bupl.dk/iwfile/BALG
-8RQDV8/$file/EnPaedagogiskHistorie.pdf.

Internal vs. external locus of control: *Wikipedia,* s.v. "locus of control,"
last modified February 11, 2016, http://en.wikipedia.org/wiki/
Locus_of_control.

Children, adults, and adolescents who exhibit the helpless feelings
associated with an external locus of control are predisposed to
anxiety and depression. Ho Cheung William Li and Oi Kwan
Joyce Chung, "The Relationship Between Children's Locus of
Control and Their Anticipatory Anxiety," *Public Health Nursing*
26, no. 2 (2009): 153–60.

Study over a fifty-year period shows a rise in external locus of control in children from 1960 to 2002. Jean M. Twenge, Liqing Zhang, and Charles Im, "It's Beyond My Control: A Cross-Temporal Meta-analysis of Increasing Externality in Locus of Control, 1960–2002," *Personality and Social Psychology Review* 8, no. 3 (2004): 308–19.

The Russian psychologist Lev Vygotsky (1896–1934) was interested in development in early childhood and how people extend their existing knowledge. He created, in his short life, a theory of learning that was strangely visionary. His thinking has, to this day, had a major influence on the scope of teaching in Danish schools. It is therefore highly relevant to familiarize yourself with Vygotsky's thinking and how it is translated in a Danish context. He is particularly known for the concept he called the "zone of proximal development." This zone covers the area of the child's independence; according to Vygotsky, it is possible for the child to know and be able to cooperate within that zone. Leif Strandberg, *Vygotskij i praksis* (Copenhagen: Akademisk Forlag, 2009).

Michael White (1948–2008), founder of the field of narrative therapy, was inspired by Lev Vygotsky's concept of the zone of proximal development. He developed maps for "scaffolding" talks, built over five questions, or inquiry categories, and supporting gradual and progressive movement through the zone of proximal development. White writes about Vygotsky: "By studying social cooperation, he observed that adult carers structure children's learning in ways that allow them to move from the familiar and the routine performance of what is possible for them to know and achieve. He described the phenomenon as a movement through a learning zone, which he called 'the zone of proximal development.' This zone marks the area where children are able to learn and achieve something on their own, and that it is possible for the child to learn and achieve, in cooperation with others."

Michael White, *Kort over Narrative Landskaber* (Maps of Narrative Practice) (Copenhagen: Hans Reitzels Forlag, 2008).

Pushing kids to read earlier isn't better. Renowned professor and developmental psychologist Dr. David Elkind, author of the bestseller *The Hurried Child*, reminds us that "there is no correlation between pushing children into early reading and later academic success." What's even more disconcerting is that children who have attended academic, rather than developmental, preschools tend to exhibit higher levels of anxiety and self-esteem issues, along with reading scores that, in the long term, are no better. Pressure and anxiety are not necessary components of a solid education for your youngster and, in fact, can have long-term negative effects. http://www.heyquitpushing.com/why-sooner-inst-better.html.

Studies on rhesus monkeys and domestic rats deprived of playmates show excessive fear or inappropriate aggression. For reviews of such play-deprivation research, see Peter LaFreniere, "Evolutionary Functions of Social Play: Life Histories, Sex Differences, and Emotion Regulation," *American Journal of Play* 3, no. 4 (2011): 464–88; S. M. Pellis, V. C. Pellis, and H. C. Bell, "The Function of Play in the Development of the Social Brain," *American Journal of Play* 2, no. 3 (2010): 278–96.

Animals allowed a playmate for even an hour a day developed more normally. S. M. Pellis and V. C. Pellis, "Rough-and-Tumble Play: Training and Using the Social Brain," in *The Oxford Handbook of the Development of Play*, ed. Peter Nathan and Anthony D. Pellegrini (Oxford, UK: Oxford University Press, 2011), 245–59; H. C. Broccard-Bell, S. M. Pellis, and B. Kolb, "Juvenile Peer Play Experience and the Development of the Orbitofrontal and Medial Prefrontal Cortex," *Behavioural Brain Research* 207, no. 1 (2010): 7–13.

Exposing the brains of baby animals to stress changes them in ways that make them less responsive to stress. Engaging in play that excites fight-or-flight instincts helps children learn how to master stress. Pellis and Pellis, "Rough-and-Tumble Play"; Pellis, Pellis, and Bell, "The Function of Play."

Individuals suffering from anxiety disorders describe losing emotional control as one of their greatest fears. David H. Barlow, *Anxiety and Its Disorders: The Nature and Treatment of Anxiety and Panic*, 2nd ed. (New York: Guilford Press, 2002).

Level of playfulness in preschoolers directly correlated with coping. I. Saunders, M. Sayer, and A. Goodale, "The Relationship Between Playfulness and Coping Skills in Preschool Children: A Pilot Study," *American Journal of Occupational Therapy* 53, no. 2 (1999): 221–6.

Adolescent boys with a higher level of playfulness had better coping skills. L. M. Hess and A. C. Bundy, "The Association Between Playfulness and Coping in Adolescents," *Physical and Occupational Therapy in Pediatrics* 23, no. 2 (2003): 5–17.

Research shows juvenile animals play in order to deal with the unexpected. Marek Spinka, Ruth C. Newberry, and Marc Bekoff, "Mammalian Play: Training for the Unexpected," *Quarterly Review of Biology* 76, no. 2 (2001): 141–68.

Children learn to deal with conflict, control, and cooperation to keep playing. LaFreniere, "Evolutionary Functions of Social Play."

Children interaction in play—they negotiate roles and rules.

Stig Broström, "Børns Lærerige Leg," *Psyke & Logos* 23 (2002): 451–69.

Stig Broström is a trained educator and Ph.D. in early childhood education. He is an associate professor at the Danish School of Education at Aarhus University.

Play Patrol exists because of collaborations between Dansk Skoleidræt (Danish School Sport) and Danish schools. Danish School Sport is a national sports organization whose main objective is to promote learning, health, and well-being through sports, play, and exercise for all students in the school. "By offering activities in the school's various arenas—i.e., immediately before and after school, in the classroom and during recess—we will, in cooperation with its schools, give students the opportunity to experience the joy of sports and physical activities. We do this based on the belief that positive experiences associated with physical activity build the foundation for good habits. And that's what makes the students more able to make healthy choices in life, today and in their future." www.legepatruljen.dk.

The practice of self-control. Lev Vygotsky, "The Role of Play in Development," in *Mind in Society: The Development of Higher Psychological Processes,* ed. Michael Cole, Vera John-Steiner, Sylvia Scribner, and Ellen Souberman (Cambridge, MA: Harvard University Press, 1978): 92–104.

Lego was dubbed "The toy of the century" by *Fortune* magazine.

Originally made in wood and then plastic.

www.visitdenmark.dk/da/danmark/design/lego-et-dansk -verdensbrand.

Learning by playing is the best way to fill young children with knowledge, say two Danish researchers. There is clear scientific evidence that children learn best through play. Pernille Hviid, professor of psychology, and Bo Stjerne Thomsen, Ph.D. in architecture and media technology and director of research and learning at the Lego Foundation. Andreas Abildlund, "Children Can Play Their Way to More Learning in School," *ScienceNordic,* June 23, 2014, http://sciencenordic.com/children-can-play-their -way-more-learning-school.

Kompan playground. www.kompan.dk.

Sensory-rich environments coupled with play promote cortical growth. Silvia Helena Cardoso and Renato M. E. Sabbatini, "Learning and Changes in the Brain," 1997, http://lecerveau .mcgill.ca/flash/capsules/articles_pdf/changes_brain.pdf.

Pediatricians in the U.S. release guidelines that say play is healthy: "Unstructured play time is more valuable for the developing brain than electronic media. Children learn to think creatively, problem solve, and develop reasoning and motor skills at early ages through unstructured, unplugged play. Free play also teaches them how to entertain themselves." http://www.aap.org/en-us/about-the-aap/aap-press-room/Pages/Babies-and-Toddlers-Should-Learn-from-Play-Not-Screens.aspx.

Extra Resources and Further Inspiration

Hans Henrik Knoop, associate professor at the Danish School of Education at Aarhus University and head of research in positive psychology.

Psychology and brain research tell us much about how education can be an exciting, professionally efficient, and creative experience. Knoop describes how to combine respect for well-being, learning, wishes, and requirements with learning and creativity. Hans Henrik Knoop, *Play, Learning, and Creativity: Why Happy Children Are Better Learners* (Copenhagen: Aschehoug, 2002).

Educators can work with play and learning—how play can be instructive and how targeted learning activities can be in the nature of play. Eva Johansson and Ingrid Samuelsson, *Lærerig leg—børns læring gennem samspil* (Frederikshavn: Dafolo, 2011).

Play and learning in everyday life. M. S. Larsen, B. Jensen, I. Johansson, T. Moser, N. Ploug, and D. Kousholt, *Forskningskortlægning og forskervurdering af skandinavisk forskning i året 2009 i institutioner for de 0-6 årige (førskolen)* (Research mapping and research assessment of Scandinavian research in 2009 in institutions for 0- to 6-year-olds [preschool]) (Copenhagen: Clearinghouse for Uddannelsesforskning, 2011), number 07, http://www.eva.dk/dagtilbud/bakspejlet/forskningskortlaegning-2009.

Bo Stjerne Thomsen, director of research and learning at the Lego Foundation, agrees that schools should use games more in education: "Children learn through play. They are curious and explore things. So they create things and share with others. There is clear scientific evidence that children learn best through play."

Associate professor of psychology Pernille Hviid emphasizes that "learning through play is the priority of the basic skills that Danish and mathematics teachers teach students today. This is not a rejection of conventional wisdom, but a chance to let it interact with the imagination. If it becomes a reality, the next generation could not just take over society, it will also be geared to develop it for the future."

Learning through play is the best way to cram knowledge into the minds of the little ones in school, says two Danish researchers at the European knowledge conference ESOF: http://videnskab .dk/miljo-naturvidenskab/born-skal-lege-sig-klogere-i-skolen.

Jennifer Freeman, David Epston, and Dean Lobovits, *Playful Approaches to Serious Problems* (New York: W. W. Norton & Company, 1997).

Chapter 3: **A** Is for Authenticity

Sad movies make you happy. S. Knobloch-Westerwick, Y. Gong, H. Hagner, and L. Kerbeykian, "Tragedy Viewers Count Their Blessings: Feeling Low on Fiction Leads to Feeling High on Life," *Communication Research* 40, no. 6 (2013): 747–66.

M. B. Oliver and A. A. Raney, "Entertainment as Pleasurable and Meaningful: Differentiating Hedonic and Eudaimonic Motivations for Entertainment Consumption," *Journal of Communication* 61, no. 5 (2011): 984–1004; Elizabeth L. Cohen, "TV So Good It

Hurts: The Psychology of Watching *Breaking Bad*," *Scientific American*, September 29, 2013, http://blogs.scientificamerican.com/guest-blog/2013/09/29/tv-so-good-it-hurts-the-psychology-of-watching-breaking-bad/.

Debate over the ending of the fairy tale "The Little Mermaid." Some scholars consider the happy ending to be an unnatural addition. http://en.wikipedia.org/wiki/The_Little_Mermaid.

To understand the feelings, thoughts, and intentions that underline the child's actions.

Janne Østergaard Hagelquist and Marianne Køhler Skov, *Mentalisering i pædagogik og terapi* (Latvia: Hans Reitzels Forlag, 2014).

Humility is not ignorance of who or what you are; rather, it's the acceptance and recognition of what is not in relationship to the other.

Article about humility and ethics in Denmark by Jacob Birkler, "Ydmyghed er en sand dyd," etik.dk, August 15, 2011, www.etik.dk/klummen-etisk-set/ydmyghed-er-en-sand-dyd.

C. S. Dweck, *Mindset: The New Psychology of Success* (New York, Random House, 2006).

C. S. Dweck, *Self-Theories: Their Role in Motivation, Personality, and Development* (Philadelphia: Taylor and Francis/Psychology Press, 1999).

L. S. Blackwell, K. H. Trzesniewski, and C. S. Dweck, "Implicit Theories of Intelligence Predict Achievement Across an Adolescent Transition: A Longitudinal Study and an Intervention," *Child Development* 78, no. 1 (2007): 246–63.

Studies on fifth-graders look at praise for intelligence and how it creates a fixed mind-set. C. M. Mueller and C. S. Dweck, "Intelligence Praise Can Undermine Motivation and Performance," *Journal of Personality and Social Psychology* 75, no. 1 (1998): 33–52.

Brain's plasticity. N. Doidge, *The Brain That Changes Itself: Stories of Personal Triumph from the Frontiers of Brain Science* (New York: Viking, 2007).

Persistence and dedication when faced with obstacles that count: K. A. Ericsson, N. Charness, P. J. Feltovich, and R. R. Hoffman, eds., *The Cambridge Handbook of Expertise and Expert Performance* (New York: Cambridge University Press, 2006).

Janet Rae-Dupree, "If You're Open to Growth, You Tend to Grow," *New York Times*, July 6, 2008, http://www.nytimes.com/2008/07/06/business/06unbox.html?_r=0.

Extra Resources and Further Inspiration

Arthur C. Brooks, "Love People, Not Pleasure," *New York Times*, July 18, 2014, http://www.nytimes.com/2014/07/20/opinion/sunday/arthur-c-brooks-love-people-not-pleasure.html?_r=1.

The resistance can be strengthened. www.psykiatrifonden.dk.

Chapter 4: **R** Is for Reframing

Realistic optimism. Resilience and success. True Grit. *Scientific American Mind*, August 2013.

"More than education, more than experience, more than training, a person's level of resilience will determine who succeeds and who fails. That's true in the cancer ward, it's true in the Olympics, and it's true in the boardroom."

Diane Coutu, "How Resilience Works," *Harvard Business Review*, May 2002.

Numerous studies show that when we deliberately reinterpret an event so that we can feel better about it, it decreases activity in the amygdala and the insula, areas of the brain that are involved in the processing of negative emotions, and increases activity in areas of the brain involved in cognitive control and adaptive integrations. A. T. Beck and G. Emery, *Anxiety Disorders and Phobias: A Cognitive Perspective* (New York: Basic Books, 1985).

T. D. Borkovec and M. A. Whisman, "Psychosocial Treatment for Generalized Anxiety Disorder," in M. Mavissakalian and R. Prien, eds., *Anxiety Disorders: Psychological and Pharmacological Treatments* (in press) (Washington, DC: American Psychiatric Press).

Angry faces. G. Sheppes, S. Scheibe, G. Suri, P. Radu, J. Blechert, and J. J. Gross, "Emotion Regulation Choice: A Conceptual Framework and Supporting Evidence," *Journal of Experimental Psychology* 143, no. 1 (2014): 163–81.

Spiders and snakes. A. A. Shurick, J. R. Hamilton, L. T. Harris, A. K. Roy, J. J. Gross, and E. A. Phelps, "Durable Effects of Cognitive Restructuring on Conditioned Fear," *Emotion* 12, no. 6 (2012): 1393–7.

We often express ourselves in a conversation with ourselves, families, and colleagues in a negatively defining way: "I'm depressed," "She is impossible," "He never listens." Svend Aage Rasmussen, *Det fjendtlige sprog—Refleksioner over udviklinger i psykiatrien* (Copenhagen: Universitetsforlaget, Fokus, 2003), 229–45.

Reframing should be in the water we drink. Anette Prehn, "The Neuroscience of Reframing & How to Do It," Udemy video, 10:48, https://www.udemy.com/the-neuroscience-of-reframing-and-how-to-do-it/.

"It is through the personal narrative, we take the lessons learned from the events in our life to us and give them meaning. It is through the personal narrative, we link our life events to sequences that unfold over time according to specific themes."

Michael White, *Narrativ teori* (The narrative perspective in therapy, 1995). (Copenhagen: Hans Reitzels Forlag, 2006), 143.

Man is interpretive by nature, and we try to make events meaningful. A narrative is like a thread that weaves events together and forms a story. Such stories are very much meant to shape our lives. By putting events together in an alternate history, we can open up new ways of seeing ourselves and the world. Alice Morgan, *Narrative samtaler* (What is narrative therapy?) (Copenhagen: Hans Reitzels Forlag, 2005).

To facilitate a process, which White calls "reauthoring," the adult can ask curious questions of the child about what he calls "action landscape" and "awareness of the landscape." In therapeutic conversations, these concepts allow the therapist to create a context in which people are able to ascribe meaning to many of the overlooked but important events in their lives. White, *Kort over narrative landskaber.*

A problem is only a problem if it is referred to as a problem. Allan Holmgren, personal conversation with the author, 2014; Annette Holmgren, *Fra terapi til pædagogik: En brugsbog i narrativ praksis* (Copenhagen: Hans Reitzels Forlag, 2010).

We want to understand meaning in action.

Jerome Bruner, *Mening i handling* (Acts of Meaning) (Århus: Forlaget Klim, 1999).

Unique outcome, also called "exception," may also be classified as initiatives. Unique outcome is always present in people's lives, but it's usually missed and lost. White, *Kort over narrative landskaber.*

To separate actions from the person is called "externalization." Externalizing helps a person dissolve or deconstruct the problem and then create stories around it resourcefully. White, *Narrativ teori*.

Talking about problems so that they become separated from the person is a linguistic practice that gives space to alternative descriptions of children so they can express themselves in a way that makes their favorite stories more accessible (*Narrativ teori*, p. 76).

Michael White and Alice Morgan, *Narrativ terapi med børn og deres familier* (Narrative therapy with children and their families) (Copenhagen: Akademisk Forlag, 2007).

"I have emphasized and illustrated the potential of externalizing conversations to (a) assist people to break from negative identity conclusions, and to (b) pave the way for the introduction of other conversations which contribute to the exploration of and generation of more positive identity conclusions. These positive identity conclusions are not stand-alone phenomena. They are associated with specific knowledges of life and practices of living."

"You can and must always tell a different story than the dominant story. Each story gives no depth, no perspective in the recital and in the description. We find it more relevant to thicken these tales than to lavish our children with superficial praise." White, *Narrativ teori* (The narrative perspective in therapy). (Copenhagen: Hans Reitzels Forlag, 2006).

Chapter 5: E Is for Empathy

Level of empathy has dropped 50 percent. S. Konrath, E. O'Brien, and C. Hsing, "Changes in Dispositional Empathy in American College Students over Time: A Meta-analysis," *Personality and Social Psychology Review* 15, no. 2 (2011): 180–98.

Narcissism has risen significantly and linearly. Jean M. Twenge and Joshua D. Foster, "Birth Cohort Increases in Narcissistic Personality Traits Among American College Students, 1982–2009," *Social Psychological and Personality Science* 1, no. 1 (2010): 99–106; Jean M. Twenge, S. Konrath, J. D. Foster, W. K. Campbell, and B. J. Bushman, "Egos Inflating over Time: A Cross-Temporal Meta-analysis of the Narcissistic Personality Inventory," *Journal of Personality* 76, no. 4 (2008): 875–902.

Peter Gray, "Why Is Narcissism Increasing Among Young Americans?" *Psychology Today*, January 16, 2014, http://www.psychologytoday.com/blog/freedom-learn/201401/why-is-narcissism-increasing-among-young-americans.

Narcissism has reached new heights. J. M. Twenge and W. K. Campbell, *The Narcissism Epidemic: Living in the Age of Entitlement* (New York: Free Press, 2009).

For many years in the U.S., we have believed that humans, like nature, are fundamentally selfish, aggressive, and competitive. Maia Szalavitz, "Is Human Nature Fundamentally Selfish or Altruistic?" *Time*, October 2012, http://healthland.time.com/2012/10/08/is-human-nature-fundamentally-selfish-or-altruistic/.

Brené Brown: "People are afraid to be vulnerable for disconnecting. . . . We are the most in debt, obese, addicted, and medicated society in the world." Brené Brown, "The Power of Vulnerability," filmed June 2010, TED video, 20:19, https://www.ted.com/talks/brene_brown_on_vulnerability.

Social brain. Matthew D. Lieberman, *Social: Why Our Brains Are Wired to Connect* (New York: Crown, 2013).

Lieberman believes that we are wired not only for self-interest but also for interest in the welfare of others. "The Social Brain and Its Superpowers: Matthew Lieberman, Ph.D. at TEDxStLouis," YouTube video, 17:58, posted by "TEDx Talks," October 7, 2013, https://www.youtube.com/watch?v=NNhk3owF7RQ&feature=kp.

Prisoner's dilemma. Robin Marantz Henig, "Linked In: 'Social,' by Matthew D. Lieberman," *New York Times*, November 1, 2013, http://www.nytimes.com/2013/11/03/books/review/social-by -matthew-d-lieberman.html?_r=1.

Empathy studies on animals. From an evolution standpoint, empathy was a valuable impulse that helped us survive in groups. Frans de Waal, *The Age of Empathy: Nature's Lessons for a Kinder Society* (New York: Harmony Books, 2009).

Greg Ross, "An Interview with Frans de Waal," *American Scientist*, http://www.americanscientist.org/bookshelf/pub/an-interview -with-frans-de-waal.

Frans de Waal, "Moral Behavior in Animals," filmed November 2011, TED video, 16:52, http://www.ted.com/talks/frans_de_waal _do_animals_have_morals.

Only when scientists began studying infants interacting with their mothers did the picture change crucially. The evidence showed that children are born with the ability to do what Professor Daniel N. Stern calls "fading"—i.e., tuning in to the mother's emotions and moods, and doing so later on with other people. This brings us back to the basics of the human capacity for empathy—the ability to empathize, to sense and understand another's feelings.

Learn more about empathy: http://www.family-lab.com/about/ jesper-juul-articles/item/empati-3.

The midbrain, or mesencephalon, contains portions of the limbic system, which you might say is the brain's chemical factory. The limbic system is very important for our social behavior and emotions. The "between brain" consists of the thalamus, hypothalamus, and pituitary gland.

Daniel Siegel, Center for Building a Culture of Empathy. http://culture ofempathy.com/References/Experts/Daniel-Siegel.htm.

"Empathy is not a luxury, it is a necessity." "Daniel Siegel and Edwin Rutsch: Dialogs on How to Build a Culture of Empathy," YouTube video, 58:22, posted by "Edwin Rutsch," October 29, 2012, http://www.youtube.com/watch?v=XIzTdXdhU0w.

The very first experience of empathy: When parents react to the child's different expressions. That way they communicate to their child that they are there and want to help.

In the first years of your child's life, your child is practicing diligently to understand and take into account other people. When she gives the doll a pacifier, puts her little brother on the knee, and plays father-mother-and-child, it is all important steps in the development of empathy. Charlotte Clemmensen: "Very young babies react to how other people feel. Studies show that infants respond to the crying from others by being scared or anxious, and some even start to cry." Charlotte Clemmensen is a trained psychologist from the Danish School of Education (Danmarks Pædagogiske Universitetskole). www.voresborn.dk/barn-3-8/psykologi-og-udvikling/4254-laer-dit-barn-at-vaere-god-mod-andre.

Eighteen-month-old toddlers show that they will almost always try to help an adult who is visibly struggling with a task. http://www.eva.mpg.de/psycho/videos/children_cabinet.mpg.

If an adult is reaching for something, the toddler will try to hand it to him, or if she sees an adult drop something accidentally, she will pick it up. On the other hand, if the same adult throws something to the ground forcefully, the toddler won't pick it up for him. F. Warneken and M. Tomasello, "Altruistic Helping in Human Infants and Young Chimpanzees," Science 311, no. 5765 (2006): 1301–3; Nathalia Gjersoe, "The Moral Life of Babies," Guardian, October 12, 2013, http://www.theguardian.com/science/2013/oct/12/babies-moral-life.

Children learn first and foremost from their parents; by using empathy and compassion, these parents pass it on to their children. www.family-lab.com/about/jesper-juul-articles/item/empati-3.

The young child learns through imitation of what is happening in the environment, and through dialogue, linking words and objects or ideas together. In the company of other kids, children are educated on the ability to read and communicate. This often occurs through imitation, body language, facial expressions, and humorous incidents. http://dcum.dk/boernemiljoe/sprog.

Types of families can affect children's ability to empathize. Jesper Juul is an internationally renowned public speaker, author, family therapist, and educator with engagements in more than fifteen countries around the globe. His findings have since been confirmed by both neuroscience and relational psychology and constitute the basis for a new paradigm and perspective in the study of and principles for dealing with families as well as the interaction between children, youth, and adults.

Jesper Juul, *Din kompetente familie* (Copenhagen: Forlaget Aprostof, 2008).

Disorders in children illustrated by the dynamic interaction between neuropsychological and developmental psychological factors. Susan Hart and Ida Møller, "Udviklingsforstyrrelser hos Børn Belyst Udfra det Dynamiske Samspil Mellem Neuropsykologiske og Udviklingspsykologiske Faktorer" (2001), www.neuroaffect.dk/Artikler_pdf/kas2.pdf.

Children from overprotective families grow up more prone to narcissism, anxiety, and depression. Rachel Sullivan, "Helicopter Parenting Causes Anxious Kids," ABC Science, August 20, 2012, http://www.abc.net.au/science/articles/2012/08/20/3570084.htm.

Cortisol affects children's brains. Sue Gerhardt, *Why Love Matters: How Affection Shapes a Baby's Brain* (New York: Routledge, 2004), 264.

Social and emotional skills can be learned just like any other skill. To be developed, they must be made visible in words and actions, supported, and recognized. One of the most important skills a child learns through childhood is to relate to others. Step by Step is a complete program designed to prevent bullying and violence, promote empathy, and develop the child's social skills. A child with social skills can master many other skills. Step by Step is an educational, systematic, logically structured, and practically applicable program to develop empathy, impulse control, and problem solving.

Step by Step (Second Step) is developed by CESEL. http://spf -nyheder.dk/download/om_cesel.pdf.

CAT-kit: www.cat-kit.com/?lan=en&area=catbox&page=catbox.

The Mary Foundation: http://www.maryfonden.dk/en.

Annie Murphy Paul, "The Protégé Effect," *Time*, November 30, 2011, http://ideas.time.com/2011/11/30/the-protege-effect/.

Studies show that there is a huge learning curve in helping others.

We know that empathy is one of the single most important factors in making successful leaders, entrepreneurs, managers, and businesses. Ashoka, "Why Empathy Is the Force That Moves Business Forward," *Forbes*, May 30, 2013, http://www.forbes.com/ sites/ashoka/2013/05/30/why-empathy-is-the-force-that-moves -business-forward/.

Empathetic teenagers are shown to be more successful because they are more purpose driven than their more narcissistic counterparts. Ugo Uche, "Are Empathetic Teenagers More Likely to Be Intentionally Successful?" *Psychology Today*, May 3, 2010, http://www.psychologytoday.com/blog/promoting-empathy -your-teen/201005/are-empathetic-teenagers-more-likely-be -intentionally.

Knud Ejler Løgstrup: www.kristeligt-dagblad.dk/debat/fasthold
-den-etiske-fodring-fortællinger-udvikler-børns-empati; www
.kristeligt-dagblad.dk/liv-sjæl/i-begyndelsen-er-tilliden.

The scenario where Lisa is playing by the sea, p. 90, is inspired by
Jesper Juul, a renowned Danish family therapist to illustrate empathy, limits, and what to do.

www.jesperjuul.com.

Studies show that reading to your children markedly increases their
empathy levels.

R. Mar, J. Tackett, and C. Moore, "Exposure to Media and
Theory-of-Mind Development in Preschoolers," *Cognitive Development* 25, no. 1 (2010): 69–78.

Having fractured relationships has been proven to cause physical and
psychological damage. Lynn E. O'Connor, "Forgiveness: When
and Why Do We Forgive," *Our Empathic Nature* (blog), *Psychology
Today*, May 21, 2012, http://www.psychologytoday.com/blog/
our-empathic-nature/201205/forgiveness-when-and-why-do-we
-forgive.

Empathy and forgiveness activate the same region of the brain.
Y. Zheng, I. D. Wilkinson, S. A. Spence, J. F. Deakin, N. Tarrier,
P. D. Griffiths, and P. W. Woodruff, "Investigating the Functional Anatomy of Empathy and Forgiveness," *Neuroreport* 12, no.
11 (2001): 2433–8.

Meaningful friend and family relationships are the most important
factors in true happiness, well above having a lot of money. Tal
Ben-Shahar, "Five Steps for Being Happier Today," Big Think
video, 1:46, 2011, http://bigthink.com/users/talbenshahar.

Chapter 6: **N** Is for No Ultimatums

Some studies suggest that up to 90 percent of Americans still use spanking at some time as a form of discipline. Karen Schrock, "Should Parents Spank Their Kids?" *Scientific American,* January 1, 2010, http://www.scientificamerican.com/article/to-spank-or -not-to-spank/.

Corporal punishment—that is, hitting students with a paddle or a cane for misbehaving—is still allowed in schools. Although it has been banned in thirty-one states, it is still allowed in private schools in all fifty states. *Wikipedia*, s.v. "school corporal punish- ment," last modified February 13, 2016, http://en.wikipedia.org/ wiki/School_corporal_punishment.

The study, which measured five different culture groups (Asian, His- panic, African American, non-Hispanic whites, and American Indian) comprising 240 focus groups in six cities across the U.S., found that all of the groups claimed, at some time or another, to use physical punishment when necessary. K. M. Lubell, T. C. Lofton, and H. H. Singer, *Promoting Healthy Parenting Practices Across Cultural Groups: A CDC Research Brief* (Atlanta: Centers for Disease Control and Prevention, National Center for Injury Pre- vention and Control, 2008).

What was even more striking were the differences across cultures in terms of when and where they spanked. Lubell, Lofton, and Singer, *Promoting Healthy Parenting Practices.*

There are four different parenting styles commonly identified in liter- ature. "Parenting Styles," Education.com, www.education.com/ reference/article/parenting-styles-2/.

D. Baumrind, "Current Patterns of Parental Authority," *Developmental Psychology Monographs* 4, no. 1, pt. 2 (1971): 1–103. Diane Baum- rind has studied the different ways in which parents raise their children.

Being a very controlling, authoritarian parent can make kids rebel. "What's Wrong with Strict Parenting?" Aha! Parenting, http://www.ahaparenting.com/parenting-tools/positive-discipline/strict-parenting.

A recent analysis covering two decades' worth of research on the long-term effects of physical punishment on children concluded that spanking not only doesn't work, but it can actually wreak havoc on kids' long-term development. Harriet L. MacMillan, Michael H. Boyle, Maria Y.-Y. Wong, Eric K. Duku, Jan E. Fleming, and Christine A. Walsh, "Slapping and Spanking in Childhood and Its Association with Lifetime Prevalence of Psychiatric Disorders in a General Population Sample," *Canadian Medical Association Journal* 161, no. 7 (1999).

There's neuroimaging evidence that physical punishment may alter parts of the brain involved in performance on IQ tests. A. Tomoda, H. Suzuki, K. Rabi, Y. S. Sheu, A. Polcari, and M. H. Teicher, "Reduced Prefrontal Cortical Gray Matter Volume in Young Adults Exposed to Harsh Corporal Punishment," *NeuroImage* 47, suppl. 2 (2009): T66–71.

Corporal punishment and substance abuse. There is data indicating that spanking can affect areas of the brain involved in emotion and stress regulation. T. O. Afifi, N. P. Mota, P. Dasiewicz, H. L. MacMillan, and J. Sareen, "Physical Punishment and Mental Disorders: Results from a Nationally Representative US Sample," *Pediatrics* 130, no. 2 (2012): 184–92.

Case in point: One mother in the George Holden study hit her toddler after the toddler either hit or kicked her, saying, "This is to help you remember not to hit your mother." "The irony is just amazing," says Holden. Bonnie Rochman, "The First Real-Time Study of Parents Spanking Their Kids," *Time*, June 28, 2011, http://healthland.time.com/2011/06/28/would-you-record-yourself-spanking-your-kids/; "The First Real-Time Study of

Parents Spanking Their Kids," YouTube video, 23:05, posted by "Stefan Molyneux," April 22, 2014, https://www.youtube.com/watch?v=N3iw0py_PL8.

Corporal punishment was gradually prohibited by law in Denmark during the twentieth century. The punishment of servants was prohibited in 1921, and in 1951 corporal punishment was abolished in public schools in Copenhagen. The "Cane Circular" of 1967 finally put an end to any form of physical punishment in Danish schools. The rights of parents to chastise their own children remained unchallenged. After the abolition of corporal punishment, violence against children became punishable under the penal code to the same extent as violence against others.

In Denmark, corporal punishment was abolished in several stages, most recently with the 1997 amendment, which clearly forbade beating children. http://da.wikipedia.org/wiki/Revselsesret.

And now more than thirty-two countries—much of Europe, Costa Rica, Israel, Tunisia, and Kenya—have similar laws. *Wikipedia*, s.v. "corporal punishment in the home," last modified February 11, 2016, http://en.wikipedia.org/wiki/Corporal_punishment_in_the_home.

Studies show children of authoritative parents are more likely to become self-reliant, socially accepted, academically successful, and well behaved. They are less likely to report depression or anxiety, and are less likely to engage in antisocial behavior such as delinquency and drug use. A. Fletcher, L. Steinberg, and E. Sellers, "Adolescents' Well-Being as a Function of Perceived Interparental Consistency," *Journal of Marriage and the Family* 61, no. 3 (1999): 599–610; E. E. Wener and R. S. Smith, *Vulnerable but Invincible: A Longitudinal Study of Resilient Children and Youth* (New York: McGraw-Hill, 1982).

Research suggests that having even one authoritative parent can make a huge difference. Fletcher, Steinberg, and Sellers, "Adolescents' Well-Being."

They are also more attuned to their parents and less influenced by their peers. D. E. Bednar and T. D. Fisher, "Peer Referencing in Adolescent Decision Making as a Function of Perceived Parenting Style," *Adolescence* 38, no. 152 (2003): 607–21.

Involving all students in getting the class to act as a socially responsible community is a process that begins in nursery school and persists when pupils leave school. This work contributes to the prevention of disorder and is also important in terms of making school bullying-free.

The school should be aware that recess is a time when children learn through play and learn to play. This is where they must learn the importance of fair play.

A paper on policy options to teaching disturbances in school: Danmarks Lærerforening, July 2009. www.dlf.org/media/97473/UroISkolen2.pdf.

Ball cushion: www.protac.dk/ball_cushion.aspx?ID=120.

Photos of balance sheets and pillow balloon: www.podconsult.dk/inklusiononline/flyers/sidderedskaber%202.pdf.

Cuddling gizmos and cots: www.familierum.dk/forside/category/dimse.

Running Laps in Schoolyards

Today, we know that physical activity is essential for the development of children's health, motor and cognitive skills, social skills, and personal identity. Since it is also a universal experience of teachers that many children experience high motivation of learning through movement, there is good reason to implement motion as a part of everyday teaching. Therefore, the Health Department, Public Health Copenhagen and Children and Youth Administration, Center for Children and Youth initiated a collaboration to develop concrete instructions and provide inspiration for how teachers in subjects such as Danish, mathematics, English, German, and history may involve movement and physical activity as a component of academic instruction. This material is called Exercise in Class: A project of Learning for All. http://playtool.dk/UserFiles/file/move_school.pdf.

Differentiate

It is a key task for the teachers to organize activities that allow individual participants linguistic challenges so all receive instruction appropriate to their current language and knowledge requirements. http://uvm.dk/Uddannelser/Uddannelser-til-voksne/Overblik-over-voksenuddannelser/Dansk-for-voksne-udlaendinge/Arbejds markedsrettet-danskundervisning/God-praksis-paa-kurser-i-arbejdsmarkedsdansk/Undervisere-Undervisningsdifferentiering.

Many teachers feel that it is a great challenge to organize an education that challenges and motivates all students. Good teaching, however, can be implemented with any student composition. www.inklusionsudvikling.dk/Vores-fire-fokusomraader/Inkluderende-laeringsfaellesskab/Laeringsmiljoer/Undervisningsdifferentiering-saa-alle-elever-udfordres-og-motiveres.

Children's Development Stages

Jean Piaget (1896–1980) was a Swiss psychologist who is known for his studies of thought processes in children. His findings have had a significant influence on contemporary teaching methods. Piaget considered the child's perception as unstable, distorted, and filled with illusions, while learning processes, or growing up, are a gradual approximation of a more orderly and systematic world of experience that helps the child to adapt to his or her environment. His theory divides development into the following stages: sensorimotor stage (0–2 years old), preoperational stage (2–6 years), concrete operational stage (6–12 years), and formal operational stage (12 and older). www.leksikon.org/art.php?n=2026.

Erik Erikson (1902–1994) was a German American psychoanalyst and developmental psychologist who believed that personality is shaped much more by the child's relationship with his or her parents than by instincts and sexuality, and it develops through a series of psychosocial stages progressing from infancy to old age.

Robert B. Ewen, *An Introduction to Theories of Personality*, 6th ed. (Mahwah, NJ: Lawrence Erlbaum Associates, 2003).

Extra Resources and Further Inspiration

Agency: a thoughtful perspective on the clarification of life by Thorkild Olsen, *Villa venire* A/S, August 2009, http://villavenire.dk/wp-content/uploads/2014/09/narrativ-metode-af-thorkild-olsen1.pdf.

Chapter 7: **T** Is for Togetherness and Hygge

Research shows that one of the top predictors of well-being and happiness is quality time with friends and family. Eric Barker, "6 Secrets You Can Learn from the Happiest People on Earth," *Time*, March 7, 2014, http://time.com/14296/6-secrets-you-can-learn-from-the-happiest-people-on-earth/; Ben-Shahar, "Five Steps."

Jeppe Trolle Linnet, from the Department of Marketing and Management at the University of Southern Denmark, is one of the few people in the world who specializes in hygge. "Hygge is not just fun. Hygge is what we identify with. Hygge is what the coming of Christmas is centered on. To hygge with other people, get the things away that distract one from the moment," he says. www.rustonline.dk/2013/12/12/hygge-i-et-seriost-lys/.

Geert Hofstede, a world-renowned cultural psychologist, concluded in a very famous study about cultural differences that the United States has the highest level of individualism in the world. Geert Hofstede, *Culture's Consequences: Comparing Values, Behaviors, Institutions, and Organizations Across Nations*, 2nd ed. (Thousand Oaks, CA: Sage Publications, 2001); Geert Hofstede, *Cultures and Organizations: Software of the Mind* (New York: McGraw-Hill, 1997).

Sushan R Sharma: "When 'I' is replaced by 'We' even 'illness' becomes 'wellness.'" SearchQuotes, s.v. "Sushan R Sharma quotes & sayings," http://www.searchquotes.com/quotes/author/Sushan_R_Sharma/5/.

A fable that illustrates substituting "we" for "I" and its effects. *Wikipedia*, s.v. "allegory of the long spoons," last modified September 25, 2015, http://en.wikipedia.org/wiki/Allegory_of_the_long_spoons.

Teamwork in Denmark. "Foreningsliv" TNS Gallup is behind the DUF (Dansk Ungdoms Fællesråd [Danish Youth Council]) (2014). www.duf.dk.

Singing and hygge. Hayley Dixon, "Choir Singing 'Boosts Your Mental Health,'" *Telegraph*, December 4, 2013, http://www.telegraph.co.uk/health/healthnews/10496056/Choir-singing-boosts-your-mental-health.html.

Researchers at Brigham Young University and the University of North Carolina at Chapel Hill pooled data from 148 studies on health outcomes and their correlation to social relationships. J. Holt-Lunstad, T. B. Smith, and J. B. Layton, "Social Relationships and Mortality Risk: A Meta-analytic Review," *PLoS Medicine* 7, no. 7 (2010): e1000316.

In another famous experiment on health and social ties, Sheldon Cohen, of Carnegie Mellon University, and colleagues exposed hundreds of healthy volunteers to the common cold virus. S. Cohen, W. J. Doyle, R. B. Turner, C. M. Alper, and D. P. Skoner, "Sociability and Susceptibility to the Common Cold," *Psychological Science* 14, no. 5 (2003): 389–95.

A research group in Chicago studied this effect and confirms it. Social support does, in fact, help manage stress. S. D. Pressman, S. Cohen, G. E. Miller, A. Barkin, B. S. Rabin, and J. J. Treanor, "Loneliness, Social Network Size, and Immune Response to Influenza Vaccination in College Freshmen," *Health Psychology* 24, no. 3 (2005): 297–306.

Research shows that people who try to be tough in a tragedy will suffer for a much longer period than those who share their emotions and are vulnerable with others.

Ben-Shahar, "Five Steps."

Yet, research shows that the reaction new mothers often have to this difficult period is to reduce the amount of social support rather than increase it. S. Joseph, T. Dalgleish, S. Thrasher, and W. Yule, "Crisis Support and Emotional Reactions Following Trauma," *Crisis Intervention & Time-Limited Treatment* 1, no. 3 (1995): 203–8.

Support from friends, family members, and parent groups has been clearly proven to help new mothers deal better with stress, thereby enabling them to see their children in a more positive light. P. A. Andersen and S. L. Telleen, "The Relationship Between Social Support and Maternal Behaviors and Attitudes: A Meta-analytic Review," *American Journal of Community Psychology* 20, no. 6 (1992): 753–74.

Extra Resources and Further Inspiration

The movie *Number Our Days* illustrates the importance of friends and loved ones around us. https://www.youtube.com/watch?v=3a ZY1IZc2MU. About Barbara Myerhoff: http://www.indiana .edu/~wanthro/theory_pages/Myerhoff.htm.

Danes want to help. According to the Charities Aid Foundation's World Giving Index, a comprehensive inventory of global charity, Denmark was in seventh place in 2012, measured by the proportion of the population who donate to charity. Approximately 70 percent of Danes donate money each year to charity. www .information.dk/455623.

Since the eighteenth edition of *Højskolesangbogens* (School song book) was published in 2006, 38,750 copies a year have been sold in Denmark. Singing is more important than ever before and reflects the Danish sing-along traditions, considered by most to have positive effects. www.kristeligt-dagblad.dk/danmark/2014 -06-21/den-danske-sangskat-er-årtiets-bogsucces.

Index

About the Authors

Iben Dissing Sandahl is a certified coach, author, and licensed narrative psychotherapist, MPF, with a private practice just outside Copenhagen, Denmark. She specializes in counseling families and children. Originally trained as a teacher, she worked for ten years in the Danish school system before earning her degree in narrative psychotherapy. She is very passionate about her work and is regularly quoted in magazines, in newspapers, and on Danish national radio for her expert opinion. She is a wife and mother of two girls, Ida and Julie. Visit www.ibensandahl.dk.

Jessica Joelle Alexander is an American author, columnist, and cultural researcher. She graduated with a B.S. in psychology and went on to teach communication and writing skills in Scandinavia and Central Europe. She has been married to a Dane for thirteen years and has always been passionate about cultural differences. She speaks four languages and lives in Rome with her husband and two children, Sophia and Sebastian. Visit www.jessicajoellealexander.com.